ANIMAL HATS

ANIMAL HATS

frog hats, elephant hats, cat hats, and more

15 Patterns
*to Knit and
Show Off*

Vanessa Mooncie

The Taunton Press

The Taunton Press
Inspiration for hands-on living®

The Taunton Press, Inc.,
63 South Main Street, PO Box 5506
Newtown, CT 06470-5506
email: tp@taunton.com

First published 2012 by
Guild of Master Craftsman
Publications Ltd
Castle Place, 166 High Street, Lewes,
East Sussex BN7 1XU

Text and designs © Vanessa Mooncie, 2012
Copyright in the Work © GMC Publications
Ltd, 2012

Library of Congress Cataloging-in-
Publication Data in progress

ISBN 978-1-60085-954-0

Publisher Jonathan Bailey
Production Manager Jim Bulley
Managing Editor Gerrie Purcell
Senior Project Editor Virginia Brehaut
Managing Art Editor Gilda Pacitti
Design Rebecca Mothersole
Photographer Chris Gloag

Set in Neo Sans
Color origination by GMC Reprographics
Printed and bound in China by Hung Hing
Printing Co. Ltd

contents

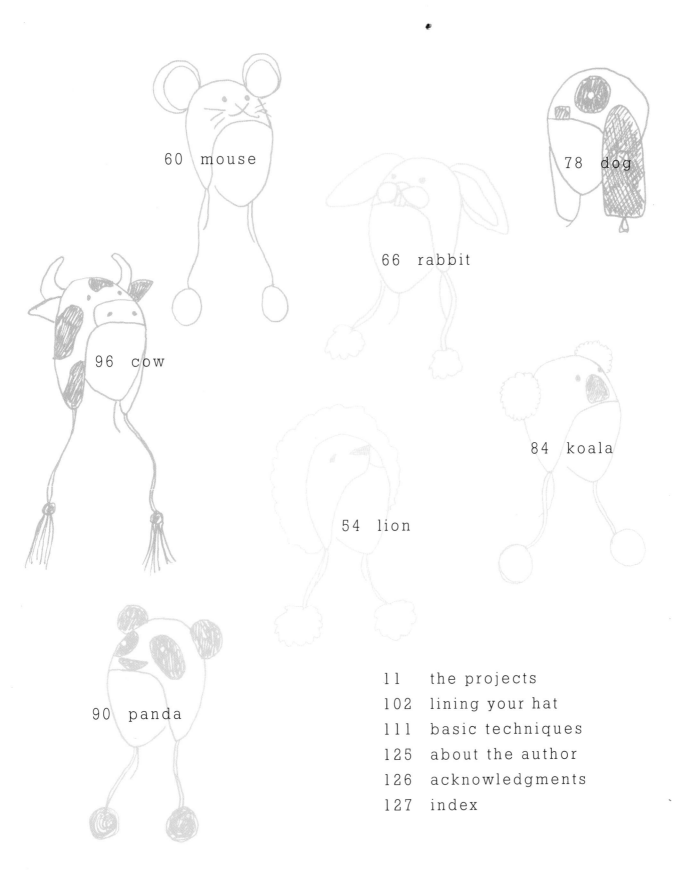

introduction

This book brings together a collection of 15 fun and unique knitted hat designs, which are aimed at both children and grown-ups. Much inspiration was drawn from historical animal apparel, such as Baby Bunting's rabbit skin in the popular nursery rhyme and the ornate animal and bird headdresses that traditionally adorned the heads of Native Americans.

Each hat project is given in a child's and an adult's size. As well as giving guidance and tips on starting the projects, each project offers two options for lining the hats to make them warm and cozy: a soft fleece fabric lining or a snuggly knitted lining.

This book of patterns will help decorate your head and keep you warm with a sense of fun, and is a must-have knitting companion for creating exuberant headwear and great handcrafted gift ideas.

the projects

chicken

Here is one hen who won't be sitting on a nest
of freshly laid eggs like her feathered friends;
this one will perch comfortably on your head, keeping
you warm and toasty on a chilly day.

MATERIALS

Wendy Merino Chunky (or equivalent), 100%
    merino wool (71yd/65m per 50g ball)
3[3] x 50g balls in 2470 Cloud (A)
1[1] x 50g ball in 2475 Poppy (B)
Approx. 7²/₃yd (7m) of any worsted-weight
    yarn in yellow for beak (C)
1 pair each of US10½/11 (7mm) and US7
    (4.5mm) knitting needles
2 x brown ¾[⅞]in (2[2.25]cm) diameter buttons
2 x black ½[⅝]in (1.25[1.5]cm) diameter buttons
Small amount of toy stuffing
Stitch holder
Tapestry needle
Sewing needle
Black sewing thread
Thin cardstock to make pompoms

SIZES

To fit: child up to 8 years [adult]

GAUGE

13 sts and 18 rows to 4in (10cm) over
stockinette stitch using US10½/11 needles.
Use larger or smaller needles if necessary to
obtain correct gauge.

OVERVIEW

The main section is knitted first. The open beak is worked in two halves, then stuffed and stitched together and attached to the front of the hat. The comb is knitted in garter stitch and shaped by decreasing and casting on stitches. The yarn is doubled to create a denser fabric, which helps the comb to stand up.

MAIN PIECE

First earflap

Both sizes

*With larger needles and A, cast on 3 sts.
Row 1 (inc) (RS): Kfb, k1, kfb (5 sts).
Row 2: K2, p1, k2.
Row 3 (inc): Kfb, k3, kfb (7 sts).
Row 4: K2, p3, k2.
Row 5 (inc): Kfb, k5, kfb (9 sts).
Row 6: K2, p5, k2.
Row 7 (inc): Kfb, k7, kfb (11 sts).
Row 8: K2, p7, k2.
Row 9 (inc): Kfb, k9, kfb (13 sts).
Row 10: K2, p9, k2.
Row 11 (inc): Kfb, k11, kfb (15 sts).
Row 12: K2, p11, k2.

Adult size only

Row 13 (inc): Kfb, k13, kfb (17 sts).
Row 14: K2, p13, k2.

Both sizes

Row 15: Knit.
Row 16: Repeat row 12[14].*
Break yarn and leave these sts on a holder.

Second earflap

Work as given for first earflap from * to *.
Next row: Cast on and k 5 sts, knit across 15[17] sts of second earflap, turn, cast on 21 sts, turn, knit across 15[17] sts of first earflap, turn, cast on 5 sts (61[65] sts).
Next row (WS): K7, p11[13], k25, p11[13], k7.
Next row: Knit.
Rep last 2 rows once more and then, starting with a purl row, work 19[21] rows in st st, ending with a WS row.

Shape crown

Row 1 (RS) (dec): K2tog, (k12[13], sl1, k2tog, psso) 3 times, k12[13], k2tog (53[57] sts).
Row 2: Purl.
Row 3 (dec): K2tog, (k10[11], sl1, k2tog, psso) 3 times, k10[11], k2tog (45[49] sts).
Row 4: Purl.
Row 5 (dec): K2tog, (k8[9], sl1, k2tog, psso) 3 times, k8[9], k2tog (37[41] sts).
Row 6: Purl.
Row 7 (dec): K2tog, (k6[7], sl1, k2tog, psso) 3 times, k6[7], k2tog (29[33] sts).
Row 8: Purl.
Row 9 (dec): K2tog, (k4[5], sl1, k2tog, psso) 3 times, k4[5], k2tog (21[25] sts).
Row 10: Purl.
Row 11 (dec): K2tog, (k2[3], sl1, k2tog, psso) 3 times, k2[3], k2tog (13[17] sts).

Adult size only

Row 12: Purl.
Row 13 (dec): K2tog, (k1, sl1, k2tog, psso) 3 times, k1, k2tog (9 sts).

Both sizes

Break yarn and thread through rem sts, draw up tight and fasten off.

EARFLAP FACING (MAKE 2)

Omit if you plan to add knitted lining

Using larger needles and A, cast on 3 sts and work rows 1 to 16 of pattern for earflaps.

Next: Rep rows 15 and 16 3 more times. Bind off loosely.

BEAK (MAKE 2)

With smaller needles and C, cast on 15[19] sts.

Adult size only

Row 1 (dec) (RS): K2tog, k6, sl1, k2tog, psso, k6, k2tog (15 sts).

Row 2: Purl.

Both sizes

Row 3 (dec): K2tog, k4, sl1, k2tog, psso, k4, k2tog (11 sts).

Row 4: Purl.

Row 5 (dec): K2tog, k2, sl1, k2tog, psso, k2, k2tog (7 sts).

Row 6: Purl.

Row 7 (dec): K2, sl1, k2tog, psso, k2 (5 sts).

Break yarn and thread through rem sts, draw up and fasten off. Sew the side seam and stuff lightly, keeping a flattened shape. Stitch both sides of the cast-on edge together to close. This makes one half of the beak.

COMB

With larger needles and B DOUBLED, cast on 9[11] sts.

Adult size only

Row 1: K7, k2tog, k2 (10 sts).

Row 2: Knit.

Row 3: K6, k2tog, k2 (9 sts).

Row 4: Knit.

Both sizes

Row 5: K5, k2tog, k2 (8 sts).

Row 6: Knit.

Row 7: K4, k2tog, k2 (7 sts).

Row 8: Knit.

Row 9: K3, k2tog, k2 (6 sts).

Row 10: Knit.

Row 11: K2, k2tog, k2 (5 sts).

Row 12: Knit.

Row 13: K1, k2tog, k2 (4 sts).

Row 14: Knit.

Row 15: Cast on and k5[7], k2tog, k2 (8[10] sts).

Rep rows 6[2]–15 then rows 6[2]–13. Bind off.

FINISHING

Using matching yarn, join the back seam.

With right sides together, sew the earflap facings to the earflaps, starting and finishing at the edge of the main section, leaving the overlapping cast-on edge open. Turn right side out and slipstitch the open edges to the inside of the main section.

Sew the comb over the center of the top of the hat from the front to the back.

Join the two halves of the beak by stitching across the bound-off edges. Sew to the center front of the hat, just above the garter-stitch border.

Make two twisted cords using A (see page 118), each measuring 8[12]in (20[30]cm) long, using 6[8] strands of yarn. Make two 2[2⅜]in (5[6]cm) pompoms in A (see page 118) and attach each to one end of the twisted cord, then stitch the other end of the cord to the tip of the earflap.

Using sewing thread, place the small black buttons over the larger brown buttons and sew in place for the eyes.

LINING THE HAT

See pages 104–109 for how to make and attach a cozy fleece or knitted lining for your hat.

frog

A pair of huge, bulging eyes and super-sized tassels
make this amazing amphibian a whole lot of fun.
The soft, super-chunky yarn makes this cold-blooded
creature extra warm and cozy.

MATERIALS

Sirdar Big Softie Super Chunky (or equivalent),
    51% wool, 49% acrylic (49yd/45m per 50g ball)
2[2] x 50g balls in 325 (A)
2[2] x 50g balls in 321 (B)
Approx. 21yd (19m) of any chunky yarn in
    white for eyeballs (C)
1 pair each of US15 (10mm) and US10½ /11
    (7mm) needles
2 x black ¾[⅞]in (2[2.25]cm) diameter buttons
2 x black ½in (1.25cm) diameter buttons
Stitch holder
Tapestry needle
Sewing needle
Black sewing thread
Small amount of toy stuffing
Thin cardstock to make tassels

SIZES

To fit: child up to 8 years [adult]

GAUGE

9 sts and 12 rows to 4in (10cm) over stockinette
stitch using US15 (10mm) needles. Use larger
or smaller needles if necessary to obtain correct
gauge.

OVERVIEW

The main section of the hat is knitted first, starting with the earflaps. The face is formed with a simple intarsia pattern with a lighter shade of green worked in garter stitch. The eyes are knitted separately, with the whites stuffed to form balls, then slipped into knitted sockets shaped like mini hats. Buttons finish the face and tassels decorate the twisted cords.

MAIN PIECE

First earflap

Both sizes

*With larger needles and A, cast on 3 sts.
Row 1 (inc) (RS): Kfb, k1, kfb (5 sts).
Row 2: K2, p1, k2.
Row 3 (inc): Kfb, k3, kfb (7 sts).

Row 4: K2, p3, k2.
Row 5 (inc): Kfb, k5, kfb (9 sts).
Row 6: K2, p5, k2.
Adult size only
Row 7 (inc): Kfb, k7, kfb (11 sts).
Row 8: K2, p7, k2.
Both sizes
Row 9: Knit.
Row 10: Repeat row 6[8].*
Break yarn and leave these sts on a holder.

Second earflap

Work as given for first earflap from * to *.
Next row: Cast on and k 4 sts, knit across 9[11] sts of second earflap, turn, cast on 15 sts, turn, knit across 9[11] sts of first earflap, turn, cast on 4 sts (41[45] sts).
Next row (WS): K6, p5[7], k19, p5[7], k6.
Next row: Knit.
Rep first of last 2 rows once more.
Work following 7 rows of intarsia from chart on page 22 or as given below:
Row 1 (RS): K6[7]A, k6[7]B, k17A, k6[7]B, k6[7]A.
Row 2: P6[7]A, k6[7]B, p17A, k6[7]B, p6[7]A.
Row 3: K4[5]A, k2B, p6[7]B, k2B, k13A, k2B, p6[7]B, k2B, k4[5]A.
Row 4: P4[5]A, k10[11]B, p13A, k10[11]B, p4[5]A.
Row 5: K2[3]A, k2B, p10[11]B, k2B, k9A, k2B, p10[11]B, k2B, k2[3]A.
Row 6: P2[3]A, k14[15]B, p9A, k14[15]B, p2[3]A.
Row 7: K2[3]A, p14[15]B, k9A, p14[15]B, k2[3]A.
Row 8: Knit with B.

Row 9: Purl with B.
Continue in yarn B.
Rep last 2 rows 3 more times, then row 8 again, to end on WS row.
Shape crown
Row 1 (dec): P2tog, (p7[8], sl1 purlwise, p2tog, psso) 3 times, p7[8], p2tog (33[37] sts).
Row 2: Knit.
Row 3 (dec): P2tog, (p5[6], sl1 purlwise, p2tog, psso) 3 times, p5[6], p2tog (25[29] sts).
Row 4: Knit.
Row 5 (dec): P2tog, (p3[4], sl1 purlwise, p2tog, psso) 3 times, p3[4], p2tog (17[21] sts).
Row 6: Knit.
Row 7 (dec): P2tog, (p1[2], sl1 purlwise, p2tog, psso) 3 times, p1[2], p2tog (9[13] sts).
Break yarn and thread through rem sts, draw up tight and fasten off.

EARFLAP FACING (MAKE 2)

Omit if you plan to add knitted lining

With larger needles and A, cast on 3 sts and work rows 1 to 10 of pattern for earflaps.
Next: Rep rows 9 and 10, 3 more times. Bind off loosely.

FROG CHART (7 rows x 41[45] sts)

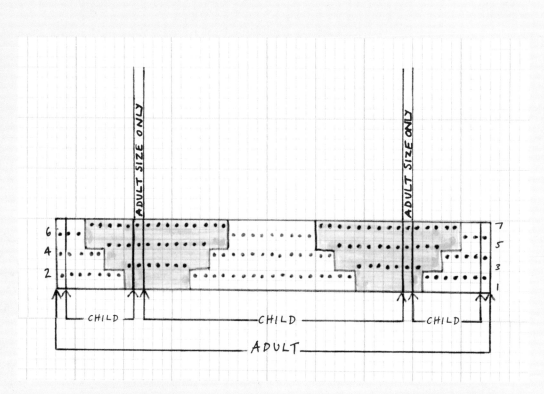

KEY

☐ KNIT
⊡ PURL
☐ YARN A
▨ YARN B

EYE SOCKETS (MAKE 2)

With larger needles and A, cast on 17[21] sts.

Starting with a k row, work 3 rows in garter st.

Row 4 (dec) (RS): (K2tog[k1], k1[k2tog]) 5[7] times k2tog[k0] (11[14] sts).

Knit 1[3] rows.

Next row (dec): (K2tog, k1) 3[4] times, k2tog (7[9] sts).

Break yarn, thread through rem sts, draw up to gather and fasten off.

FINISHING

Using matching yarn, join the back seam.

With right sides together, sew the earflap facings to the earflaps, starting and finishing at the edge of the main section, leaving the overlapping cast-on edge open. Turn right side out and slipstitch the open edges to the inside of the main section.

With right sides together, sew the back seam of the eyeball. Turn right side out and stuff to form a ball shape before running a gathering st around the cast-on edge to close.

Join the seam of the eye socket. Slip the eyeball inside so the seam is at the back and the gathered ends are hidden inside the socket. Stitch carefully in place. Attach to the main section of the hat so the seam of the socket is facing down.

EYEBALLS (MAKE 2)

With smaller needles and C, cast on 9 sts.

Row 1 (inc): (K1, kfb) 4 times, k1 (13 sts).

Adult size only

Row 2: Purl.

Row 3 (inc): (K1, kfb) 6 times, k1 (19 sts).

Both sizes

Starting with a p row, work 5[7] rows in st st.

Adult size only

Row 13 (dec): (K1, k2tog) 6 times, k1 (13 sts).

Row 14: Purl.

Both sizes

Row 15 (dec): (K1, k2tog) 4 times, k1 (9 sts).

Break yarn and thread through rem sts, draw up to gather and fasten off.

Make two twisted cords using A (see page 118), each measuring 8[12]in (20[30]cm) long, using 4[6] strands of yarn. Make two tassels (see page 119) measuring 4[5⅛]in (10[13]cm) long in B, and attach each to one end of the twisted cord, then stitch the other end of the cord to the tip of the earflap.

Using sewing thread, sew the large buttons to the middle of the eyeballs and the small buttons in place at the front of the hat for the nostrils.

LINING THE HAT

See pages 104–109 for how to make and attach a cozy fleece or knitted lining for your hat.

penguin

With his wooly wings to warm your ears, this smart, suited penguin has a bow tie with a little sparkle. The tie can be pinned onto the hat or, alternatively, used to dress up your own shirt collar.

MATERIALS

Twilleys Freedom Purity Chunky (or equivalent), 85%
    wool, 15% alpaca (79yd/72m per 50g ball)
3[3] x 50g balls in 785 Coal (A)
1[1] x 50g ball in 787 Limestone (B)
Rowan Shimmer (or equivalent), 60% cupro,
    40% polyester (191yd/175m per 25g ball)
1[1] x 25g ball in 095 Jet (C)
Approx. 5½yd (5m) of any worsted yarn in
    black for beak (D)
1 pair each of US10½ /11 (7mm) and
    US6 (4mm) needles
2 x blue or white ⅞in (2.25cm) diameter buttons
2 x black ⅞in (2.25cm) diameter buttons
2 x black ⅝in (1.5cm) diameter buttons
Tapestry needle
Sewing needle
Black sewing thread
Pin back (found in the jewelry section of craft
    and hobby stores)
Small amount of toy stuffing

SIZES

To fit: child up to 8 years [adult]

GAUGE

13 sts and 18 rows to 4in (10cm) over stockinette
stitch using US10½ /11 (7mm) needles. Use
larger or smaller needles if necessary to obtain
correct gauge.

OVERVIEW

The main piece is in a simple intarsia design. The wings and beak are knitted separately, and buttons are added for eyes and to fasten the wings up for an alternative look. A pin back allows the bow tie to be pinned where preferred.

WING FACINGS (MAKE 2)

Both sizes

Using larger needles and A, cast on 5 sts.
Row 1 (RS) (inc): Kfb, k3, kfb (7 sts).
Row 2: Knit.
Row 3 (inc): Kfb, k5, kfb (9 sts).
Row 4: Knit.
Row 5 (inc): Kfb, k7, kfb (11 sts).
Row 6: Knit.
Row 7 (inc): Kfb, k9, kfb (13 sts).

Adult size only

Row 8: Knit.
Row 9 (inc): Kfb, k11, kfb (15 sts).

Both sizes

Continue without shaping in garter st (k every row) until work measures 4¾[6] in (12[15]cm) from cast-on edge, ending with a WS row. Break yarn and leave these sts on a holder.

MAIN PIECE

The following is worked in intarsia:
Using larger needles and A, cast on 8 sts, turn and knit across 13[15] sts of one ear facing, turn. Join in B and cast on 19 sts, turn and knit across 13[15] sts of other ear facing in A, turn and cast on 8 sts in A (61[65] sts).
Next row: K21[23]A, k19B, k21[23]A.
Rep last row 3 more times.
Next row (WS): P21[23]A, p19B, p21[23]A.
Next row (RS): K21[23]A, k19B, k21[23]A.
Rep last 2 rows 4 times more, then first of the previous 2 rows once again to end with a WS row.

Adult size only

Work 2 more rows.

Both sizes

Work next 8 rows in patt from the chart or as given below:
Row 1: K22[24]A, k7B, k3A, k7B, k22[24]A.
Row 2: P22[24]A, p7B, p3A, p7B, p22[24]A.
Row 3: K22[24]A, k6B, k5A, k6B, k22[24]A.
Row 4: P22[24]A, p6B, p5A, p6B, p22[24]A.
Row 5: K23[25]A, k4B, k7A, k4B, k23[25]A.
Row 6: P23[25]A, p4B, p7A, p4B, p23[25]A.
Row 7: Knit with A.
Row 8: Purl with A.

Shape crown

Row 1 (RS) (dec): K2tog, k11[12], sl1, k2tog, psso, (k13[14], sl1, k2tog, psso) twice, k11[12], k2tog (53[57] sts).
Row 2: Purl.
Row 3 (dec): K2tog, k9[10], sl1, k2tog, psso, (k11[12], sl1, k2tog, psso) twice, k9[10], k2tog (45[49] sts).
Row 4: Purl.
Row 5 (dec): K2tog, k7[8], sl1, k2tog, psso, (k9[10], sl1, k2tog, psso) twice, k7[8], k2tog (37[41] sts).
Row 6: Purl.
Row 7 (dec): K2tog, k5[6], sl1, k2tog, psso, (k7[8], sl1, k2tog, psso) twice, k5[6], k2tog (29[33] sts).
Row 8: Purl.
Row 9 (dec): K2tog, k3[4], sl1, k2tog, psso, (k5[6], sl1, k2tog, psso) twice, k3[4], k2tog (21[25] sts).
Row 10: Purl.
Row 11 (dec): K2tog, k1[2], sl1, k2tog, psso, (k3[4], sl1, k2tog, psso) twice, k1[2], k2tog (13[17] sts).

Adult size only

Row 12: Purl.
Row 13 (dec): K2tog, sl1, k2tog, psso, (k2, sl1, k2tog, psso) twice, k2tog (9 sts).

Both sizes

Break yarn and thread through rem sts, draw up tight and fasten off.

PENGUIN CHART (8 rows x 61[65] sts)

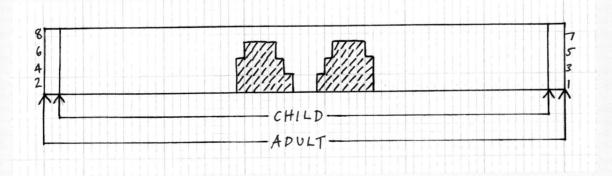

KEY

□ YARN A
▨ YARN B

WINGS (MAKE 2)
Both sizes
Using larger needles and B, cast on 3 sts, (pass previous st over st just made, slipping it off the needle, cast on 1) 3 times to make buttonhole.

Row 1 (WS): K1, turn, cast on 3 sts, turn, k1 (5 sts).

Row 2 (RS) (inc): Kfb, k3, kfb (7 sts).

Row 3: Knit.

Row 4 (inc): Kfb, k5, kfb (9 sts).

Row 5: Knit.

Row 6 (inc): Kfb, k7, kfb (11 sts).

Row 7: Knit.

Row 8 (inc): Kfb, k9, kfb (13 sts).

Adult size only
Row 9: Knit.

Row 10 (inc): Kfb, k11, kfb (15 sts).

Both sizes
Continue in garter st until work measures 7[8¼]in (18[21]cm) from cast-on edge of row 1, ending with a WS row.

Shape top
Next row (dec): K1, k2tog, k to last 3 sts, k2tog, k1.

Next row: Knit.

Rep last 2 rows until 9 sts rem, then rep the first of the last 2 rows once more (7 sts).

Bind off 7 sts.

BEAK
Both sizes
With smaller needles and C and D worked together, cast on 21 sts.

Row 1 (dec): K2tog, k7, sl1, k2tog, psso, k7, k2tog (17 sts).

Row 2: Purl.

Row 3 (dec): K2tog, k5, sl1, k2tog, psso, k5, k2tog (13 sts).

Row 4: Purl.

Row 5 (dec): K2tog, k3, sl1, k2tog, psso, k3, k2tog (9 sts).

Row 6: Purl.

Row 7 (dec): K2tog, k1, sl1, k2tog, psso, k1, k2tog (5 sts).

Break yarn and thread through rem sts, draw up and fasten off.

BOW TIE
Both sizes
With larger needles and A and C worked together, cast on 8 sts.

Work in garter st for 7in (18cm).

Bind off.

KNOT
With larger needles and A and C worked together, cast on 4 sts.

Work 10 rows in garter st.

Bind off.

FINISHING
Using matching yarn, join the back seam of main section.

Position the wrong side of wings over right side of facings and hat. Slipstitch in place, leaving the buttonholes free.

Join the seam of the beak to form a cone and stuff before attaching to the center front of the hat, just below the point where yarn A meets yarn B, with the seam facing downward.

Using sewing thread, sew a large black button to the top of each wing. Place the small black buttons over the blue or white buttons and stitch to the main section for the eyes.

Fold the main part of the bow tie in half and join the short edges. Place the seam of the bow tie at the center back. Wrap the knot around the center of the main piece, covering the seam. Join the short edges of the knot and sew in place. This will pull in the middle of the main piece to give the effect of a bow. Sew a pin back to the back of the bow tie. Pin to the front of the penguin.

LINING THE HAT
See pages 104–109 for how to make and attach a cozy fleece or knitted lining for your hat.

elephant

While elephants' ears keep them cool, this hat will
keep the wearer warm and protected from the elements.
The tweed yarn with flecks of bright hues running
through it adds tiny touches of color.

MATERIALS

Sublime Chunky Merino Tweed (or equivalent),
    80% wool, 10% viscose, 10% acrylic
    (87yd/80m per 50g ball)
4[4] x 50g balls in 235 Pigeon (A)
Sublime Extra Fine Merino Wool DK (or equivalent),
    100% merino wool (127yd/116m per 50g ball)
1[1] x 50g balls in 003 Alabaster (B)
1 pair each of US10½ /11 (7mm) and
    US6 (4mm) needles
2 x white ¾[⅞]in (2[2.25]cm) diameter buttons
2 x black ½[⅝]in (1.25[1.5]cm) diameter buttons
Small amount of toy stuffing
Stitch holder
Tapestry needle
Sewing needle
Black sewing thread
Thin cardstock to make tassels

SIZES

To fit: child up to 8 years [adult]

GAUGE

13 sts and 18 rows to 4in (10cm) over stockinette
stitch using US10½ /11 (7mm) needles. Use
larger or smaller needles if necessary to obtain
correct gauge.

OVERVIEW

The hat is knitted in stockinette stitch, starting with the triangular earflaps. The ears are in garter stitch, lightly stuffed and stitched to the main part. The trunk and tusks are worked with the yarn doubled to create a firmer fabric. The elephant is finished with button eyes and tassels hanging from twisted cords.

MAIN PIECE

First earflap

Both sizes

*With larger needles and A, cast on 3 sts.

Row 1 (inc) (RS): Kfb, k1, kfb (5 sts).

Row 2: K2, p1, k2.

Row 3 (inc): Kfb, k3, kfb (7 sts).

Row 4: K2, p3, k2.

Row 5 (inc): Kfb, k5, kfb (9 sts).

Row 6: K2, p5, k2.

Row 7 (inc): Kfb, k7, kfb (11 sts).

Row 8: K2, p7, k2.

Row 9 (inc): Kfb, k9, kfb (13 sts).

Row 10: K2, p9, k2.

Row 11 (inc): Kfb, k11, kfb (15 sts).

Row 12: K2, p11, k2.

Adult size only

Row 13 (inc): Kfb, k13, kfb (17 sts).

Row 14: K2, p13, k2.

Both sizes

Row 15: Knit.

Row 16: As row 12[14].*

Break yarn and leave these sts on a holder.

Second earflap

Work as given for first earflap from * to *.

Next row: Cast on and k 5 sts, knit across 15[17] sts of second earflap, turn, cast on 21 sts, turn, knit across 15[17] sts of first earflap, turn, cast on 5 sts (61[65] sts).

Next row (WS): K7, p11[13], k25, p11[13], k7.

Next row: Knit.

Rep last 2 rows once more and then, starting with a purl row, work 19[21] rows in st st, ending with a WS row.

Shape crown

Row 1 (RS) (dec): K2tog, (k12[13], sl1, k2tog, psso) 3 times, k12[13], k2tog (53[57] sts).

Row 2: Purl.

Row 3 (dec): K2tog, (k10[11], sl1, k2tog, psso) 3 times, k10[11], k2tog (45[49] sts).

Row 4: Purl.

Row 5 (dec): K2tog, (k8[9], sl1, k2tog, psso) 3 times, k8[9], k2tog (37[41] sts).

Row 6: Purl.

Row 7 (dec): K2tog, (k6[7], sl1, k2tog, psso) 3 times, k6[7], k2tog (29[33] sts).

Row 8: Purl.

Row 9 (dec): K2tog, (k4[5], sl1, k2tog, psso) 3 times, k4[5], k2tog (21[25] sts).

Row 10: Purl.

Row 11 (dec): K2tog, (k2[3], sl1, k2tog, psso) 3 times, k2[3], k2tog (13[17] sts).

Adult size only

Row 12: Purl.

Row 13 (dec): K2tog, (k1, sl1, k2tog, psso) 3 times, k1, k2tog (9 sts).

Both sizes

Break yarn and thread through rem sts, draw up tight and fasten off.

EARFLAP FACING (MAKE 2)

Omit if you plan to add knitted lining

Using larger needles and A, cast on 3 sts and work as for earflaps.

Next: Rep rows 15 and 16, 3 more times. Bind off loosely.

OUTER EAR (MAKE 2)

With larger needles and A, cast on 12[14] sts.

Rows 1–2: Knit.

Row 3 (inc): Kfb, k to last st, kfb (14[16] sts).

Row 4 (inc): Kfb, k to end (15[17] sts).

Rep last 2 rows until there are 21[23] sts.

Next row (inc): K to last st, kfb (22[24] sts).

Next row (inc): Kfb, k to end (23[25] sts).

K1[3] rows without shaping.

Next row (dec): K2tog, k to end (22[24] sts).

Next row (dec): K to last 2 sts, k2tog (21[23] sts).

Rep last 2 rows once more (19[21] sts).

Next row (dec): K2tog, k to end (18[20] sts).

Next row (dec): K2tog, k to last 2 sts, k2tog (16[18] sts).

Next row (dec): K2tog, k to end (15[17] sts).

Rep last 2 rows twice more (9[11] sts).

Next row (dec): K2tog, k to last 2 sts, k2tog (7[9] sts).

Adult size only

Next row (dec): K2tog, k to last 2 sts, k2tog (7 sts).

Both sizes. Bind off.

34

INNER EAR (MAKE 2)
Work as given for outer ear.

TRUNK
With larger needles and A DOUBLED, cast on 19[21] sts.

Row 1 (dec): K2tog, k to last 2 sts, k2tog (17[19] sts).

Row 2: Purl.

Row 3: Kfb, k6[7], sl1, k2tog, psso, k6[7], kfb.

Row 4: Purl.

Rep last 2 rows twice more.

Row 9: As row 3.

Row 10: Kfb, p6[7], p2tog, slip the stitch just worked onto the left-hand needle and pass the next st over it, slip the stitch back onto the right-hand needle, p6[7], kfb.

Rep last 2 rows 5 more times.

Row 21 (dec): K7[8], sl1, k2tog, psso, k7[8] (15[17] sts).

Row 22: Purl.

Adult size only

Row 23 (dec): K7, sl1, k2tog, psso, k7 (15 sts).

Row 24: Purl.

Shape top

Both sizes

Next row: Bind off 4 sts, k to end (11 sts).

Next row: Bind off 4 sts, p to end (7 sts).

Next row (dec): K2tog, k3, k2tog (5 sts).

Next row: Purl.

Next row (dec): K2tog, k1, k2tog (3 sts).

Next row: Purl.

Next row: Sl1, k2tog, psso.

Fasten off.

TUSKS (MAKE 2)
With smaller needles and B DOUBLED, cast on 17[19] sts.

Row 1 (dec): K2tog, k to last 2 sts, k2tog (15[17] sts).

Row 2: Purl.

Row 3 (dec): K2tog, k to last 2 sts, k2tog (13[15] sts).

Row 4: Purl.

Row 5 (dec): K5[6], sl1, k2tog, psso, k5[6] (11[13] sts).

Row 6: Purl.

Row 7: Kfb, k3[4], sl1, k2tog, psso, k3[4], kfb.

Row 8: Purl.

Rep last 2 rows 2[3] times more.

Next row (dec): K4[5], sl1, k2tog, psso, k4[5] (9[11] sts).

Next row: Purl.

Next row (dec): K2tog, k1[2], sl 1, k2tog, psso, k1[2], k2tog (5[7] sts).

Break yarn and thread through rem sts. Fasten off.

FINISHING
Using matching yarn, join the back seam.

With right sides together, sew the earflap facings to the earflaps, starting and finishing at the edge of the main section, leaving the overlapping cast-on edge open. Turn right side out and slipstitch the open edges to the inside of the main section.

With right sides together, join the two ear pieces, leaving an opening. Turn the work right side out and stuff lightly, keeping the flattened shape, then sew closed. Attach the cast-on edges to each side of the hat with the pointed end of the ear facing down.

With right sides together, fold the trunk, matching the seams. Stitch from the pointed V-shaped tip down the length of the seam, leaving the cast-on edge open. Stuff the trunk firmly, using a knitting needle to push the stuffing right into the ends. Attach the trunk to the hat, stitching all around the cast-on edge and work a few stitches near the end of the trunk to keep it in place at the top of the hat. Join the curved seam of the tusks. Stuff firmly and attach to either side of the trunk.

Make two twisted cords using A (see page 118), each measuring 8[12]in (20[30]cm) long, using 6[8] strands of yarn. Make two tassels (see page 119) measuring 4[5⅛]in (10[13]cm) long in A, and attach each to one end of the twisted cord, then stitch the other end of the cord to the tip of the earflap.

Using sewing thread, place the small black buttons over the larger white buttons and sew in place for the eyes.

LINING THE HAT
See pages 104–109 for how to make and attach a cozy fleece or knitted lining for your hat.

monkey

This cheeky chap is knitted in subtle shades of brown and gray bouclé yarn, which can easily be replaced by strong, contrasting colors and other textures to create an altogether different character.

MATERIALS

Any bouclé or textured chunky yarn

3[3] x 50g balls in brown (A)

1[1] x 50g balls in gray (B)

1 pair of US10 (6mm) needles

2 x brown ¾[⅞]in (2[2.25]cm) diameter buttons

2 x black ½[⅝]in (1.25[1.5]cm) diameter buttons

Stitch holder

Tapestry needle

Sewing needle

Black sewing thread

Small amount of toy stuffing

Thin cardstock to make tassels

SIZES

To fit: child up to 8 years [adult]

GAUGE

13 sts and 18 rows to 4in (10cm) over stockinette stitch using US10 (6mm) needles. Use larger or smaller needles if necessary to obtain correct gauge.

OVERVIEW

The monkey's ears and face are knitted separately and attached to the finished main section. The lower part of the face is stuffed lightly to give it shape. Nostrils are embroidered and the hat is finished with twisted cords and big tassels.

MAIN PIECE

First earflap

Both sizes

*With A, cast on 3 sts.

Row 1 (inc) (RS): Kfb, k1, kfb (5 sts).
Row 2: K2, p1, k2.
Row 3 (inc): Kfb, k3, kfb (7 sts).
Row 4: K2, p3, k2.
Row 5 (inc): Kfb, k5, kfb (9 sts).
Row 6: K2, p5, k2.
Row 7 (inc): Kfb, k7, kfb (11 sts).
Row 8: K2, p7, k2.
Row 9 (inc): Kfb, k9, kfb (13 sts).
Row 10: K2, p9, k2.
Row 11 (inc): Kfb, k11, kfb (15 sts).
Row 12: K2, p11, k2.

Adult size only

Row 13 (inc): Kfb, k13, kfb (17 sts).
Row 14: K2, p13, k2.

Both sizes

Row 15: Knit.
Row 16: As row 12[14].*

Break yarn and leave these sts on a holder.

Second earflap

Work as given for first earflap from * to *.

Next row: Cast on and k5 sts, knit across 15[17] sts of second earflap, turn, cast on 21 sts, turn, knit across 15[17] sts of first earflap, turn, cast on 5 sts (61[65] sts).
Next row (WS): K7, p11[13], k25, p11[13], k7.
Next row: Knit.

Rep last 2 rows once more and then starting with a purl row, work 19[21] rows in st st, ending with a WS row.

Shape crown

Row 1 (RS) (dec): K2tog, (k12[13], sl1, k2tog, psso) 3 times, k12[13], k2tog (53[57] sts).
Row 2: Purl.
Row 3 (dec): K2tog, (k10[11], sl1, k2tog, psso) 3 times, k10[11], k2tog (45[49] sts).
Row 4: Purl.
Row 5 (dec): K2tog, (k8[9], sl1, k2tog, psso) 3 times, k8[9], k2tog (37[41] sts).
Row 6: Purl.
Row 7 (dec): K2tog, (k6[7], sl1, k2tog, psso) 3 times, k6[7], k2tog (29[33] sts).
Row 8: Purl.
Row 9 (dec): K2tog, (k4[5], sl1, k2tog, psso) 3 times, k4[5], k2tog (21[25] sts).
Row 10: Purl.
Row 11 (dec): K2tog, (k2[3], sl1, k2tog, psso) 3 times, k2[3], k2tog (13[17] sts).

Adult size only

Row 12: Purl.
Row 13 (dec): K2tog, (k1, sl1, k2tog, psso) 3 times, k1, k2tog (9 sts).

Both sizes

Break yarn and thread through rem sts, draw up tight and fasten off.

EARFLAP FACING (MAKE 2)

Omit if you plan to add knitted lining

With A, cast on 3 sts and work as for earflaps.

Next: Rep rows 15 and 16, 3 more times. Bind off loosely.

FACE

Starting at the chin, with B, cast on 11[13] sts.

Row 1 (RS): Knit.
Row 2 (inc): Kfb, k9[11], kfb (13[15] sts).
Row 3: Knit.
Row 4 (inc): Kfb, k11[13], kfb (15[17] sts).

Mouth

Row 5: K2B, join in A and k11[13]A, k2B.
Row 6: K2B, k11[13]A, k2B.

Continue in B.

Rows 7-8: Knit.
Row 9 (dec): K2tog, k11[13], k2tog (13[15] sts).
Row 10: Knit.
Row 11 (dec): K2tog, k9[11] k2tog (11[13] sts).
Row 12: Knit.
Row 13 (inc): Kfb, k9[11], kfb (13[15] sts).
Row 14: Purl.
Row 15 (inc): Kfb, k5[6], kfb, k5[6], kfb (16[18] sts).
Row 16: Purl.

Adult size only

Row 17 (inc): Kfb, k16, kfb (20 sts).
Row 18: Purl.

Shape top of face
Both sizes
Each side is worked separately.
Row 19 (dec): K2tog, k4[6], k2tog, turn (6[8] sts).
Row 20: P6[8].
Row 21 (dec): K2tog, k2[4], k2tog, turn (4[6] sts).
Row 22: P4[6].
Bind off 4[6] sts. With RS facing, rejoin yarn to rem sts and work rows 19 to 22 to match first side.
Bind off.

OUTER EAR (MAKE 2)
With A, cast on 5[7] sts.
Row 1 (inc) (WS): Kfb, k3[5], kfb (7[9] sts).
Row 2 (RS): Knit.
Row 3 (inc): Kfb, k5[7], kfb (9[11] sts).
Both sizes
Work 10[12] rows in garter st.
Bind off.

INNER EAR (MAKE 2)
Work as for outer ear using yarn B.

FINISHING
Using matching yarn, join the back seam.

With right sides together, sew the earflap facings to the earflaps, starting and finishing at the edge of the main section, leaving the overlapping cast-on edge open. Turn right side out and slipstitch the open edges to the inside of the main section.

Pin the face in position to the front of the hat with the cast-on stitches sitting just above the garter-stitch edge. Slipstitch around the shaped top and then work a row of backstitch across the middle at the narrowest part. Slipstitch the remaining half of the face to the main part leaving an opening. Stuff the lower half lightly to give the mouth and chin some shape. Close the opening and fasten off neatly.

With right sides together, sew the inner to the outer ear, leaving lower edge open. Turn right side out and lightly stuff, keeping the flattened shape. Join the bound-off edges. Attach the ears to the main section of the hat so they are in line with the top shaping of the face. Stitch all around the lower edges to help prevent them flopping over.

Make two twisted cords using A (see page 118), each measuring 8[12]in (20[30]cm) long, using 6[8] strands of yarn. Make two tassels (see page 119) measuring 4[5⅛]in (10[13]cm) long in B, and attach each to one end of the twisted cord, then stitch the other end of the cord to the tip of the earflap.

Embroider a couple of French knots (see page 119) for nostrils using yarn A. Using sewing thread, place the small black buttons over the larger brown buttons and sew in place for the eyes.

LINING THE HAT
See pages 104–109 for how to make and attach a cozy fleece or knitted lining for your hat.

pig

Pretty in pink, this little piggy is knitted in soft, chunky
wool with a deep, turned-up rib to keep you extra cozy.
It is sure to chase away the winter blues.

MATERIALS

Debbie Bliss Rialto Chunky (or equivalent),
    100% extra fine merino wool (65yd/60m
    per 50g ball)
3[3] x 50g balls in 016 Brighton Rock (A)
1 pair each of US10½ (6.5mm) and
    US10½/11 (7mm) needles
2 x white ¾[⅞]in (2[2.25]cm) diameter buttons
2 x black ½[⅝]in (1.25[1.5]cm) diameter buttons
2 small black buttons for nostrils measuring around
    ½in (1.25cm) across
Small amount of toy stuffing
Tapestry needle
Sewing needle
Black sewing thread

SIZES

To fit: child up to 8 years [adult]

GAUGE

13 sts and 18 rows to 4in (10cm) over stockinette
stitch using US10½/11 (7mm) needles. Use
larger or smaller needles if necessary to obtain
correct gauge.

OVERVIEW

The main part of the hat pattern is worked in the same format as the other projects, with a 2 x 2 rib replacing the earflaps. The ears, snout, and tail are knitted separately and attached at the end.

MAIN PIECE

With smaller needles and A, cast on 60[64] sts.
Work 4½[5]in (11.5[12.75]cm) in k2, p2 rib.
Change to larger needles.
Next row (inc) (RS): Kfb, k to end (61[65] sts).
Starting with a purl row, work in st st for 15[17] rows, ending with a WS row.
Shape crown
Row 1 (RS) (dec): K2tog, (k12[13], sl1, k2tog, psso) 3 times, k12[13], k2tog (53[57] sts).
Row 2: Purl.
Row 3 (dec): K2tog, (k10[11], sl1, k2tog, psso) 3 times, k10[11], k2tog (45[49] sts).
Row 4: Purl.
Row 5 (dec): K2tog, (k8[9], sl1, k2tog, psso) 3 times, k8[9], k2tog (37[41] sts).
Row 6: Purl.
Row 7 (dec): K2tog, (k6[7], sl1, k2tog, psso) 3 times, k6[7], k2tog (29[33] sts).
Row 8: Purl.
Row 9 (dec): K2tog, (k4[5], sl1, k2tog, psso) 3 times, k4[5], k2tog (21[25] sts).
Row 10: Purl.
Row 11 (dec): K2tog, (k2[3], sl1, k2tog, psso) 3 times, k2[3], k2tog (13[17] sts).

Adult size only
Row 12: Purl.
Row 13 (dec): K2tog, (k1, sl1, k2tog, psso) 3 times, k1, k2tog (9 sts).
Both sizes
Break yarn and thread through rem sts, draw up tight and fasten off.

EARS (MAKE 2)

With larger needles and A, cast on 6 sts.
Row 1 (inc): Kfb, k1, (kfb) twice, k1, kfb (10 sts).
Row 2 (inc): Kfb, k3, (kfb) twice, k3, kfb (14 sts).
Row 3 (inc): Kfb, k5, (kfb) twice, k5, kfb (18 sts).

Row 4 (inc): Kfb, k7, (kfb) twice, k7 kfb (22 sts).
Row 5 (inc): Kfb, k9, (kfb) twice, k9, kfb (26 sts).
Row 6 (inc): Kfb, k11, (kfb) twice, k11, kfb (30 sts).
Adult size only
Row 7 (inc): Kfb, k13, (kfb) twice, k13, kfb (34 sts).
Both sizes
Work 11[15] rows in garter st. Bind off.

SNOUT

Starting at back, with larger needles and A, cast on 5[7] sts.
Row 1 (inc): (K1, kfb) 2[3] times, k1 (7[10] sts).
Row 2: Purl.
Row 3 (inc): (K1, kfb[(kfb) twice]) 3 times, k1 (10[16] sts).
Adult size only
Row 4: Purl.
Row 5 (inc): K1, ((kfb) twice, k2) 3 times, (kfb) twice, k1 (24 sts).
Both sizes
Work 3[5] rows in st st.
Adult size only
Row 11 (dec): K1, ((k2tog) twice, k2) 3 times, (k2tog) twice, k1 (16 sts).
Row 12: Purl.
Both sizes
Row 13 (dec): (K1, k2tog[(k2tog) twice]) 3 times, k1 (7[10] sts).
Row 14: Purl.
Row 15 (dec): (K1, k2tog) 2[3] times, k1 (5[7] sts). Break yarn and thread through rem sts, draw up tight and fasten off.

CURLY TAIL

Both sizes

With larger needles and A, cast on 18[22] sts loosely by inserting the needle through the last stitch made, instead of in between the last 2 sts. Change to smaller needle and bind off tightly.

FINISHING

With right sides together, and using matching yarn, join the back seam from the top of the crown to halfway down the rib, then reverse the seam with wrong sides together for the turnback.

Join seam of the snout leaving an opening and stuff the piece lightly. Close the opening. Sew the small buttons to the snout, stitching right through to the back of the work, pulling tight on the thread to draw the nostrils in. Attach snout to the main part of the hat at the center front, just above the garter-stitch border.

Fold the ear with right sides together and sew the side seam. Turn right side out and join the bound-off edges. Bring the two corners of each side from the lower edge of the ear to the middle to shape. Stitch to hold in place. Attach to the main section of the hat.

Using sewing thread, place the small black buttons over the larger white buttons and sew in place for the eyes.

Stitch tail to center back of hat above the rib.

LINING THE HAT

See pages 104–109 for how to make and attach a cozy fleece or knitted lining for your hat.

fox

This foxy fellow, with his creamy features worked in
intarsia, looks dashing in his rusty-red coat.
A shiny lurex nose, soft mohair ears, and fox-tail of
pompom-tipped cords all add to his character.

MATERIALS

Debbie Bliss Rialto Chunky (or equivalent),
    100% merino wool (65yd/60m per 50g ball)
3[3] x 50g balls in 005 Burnt Umber (A)
1[2] x 50g balls in 003 Ecru (B)
*Debbie Bliss Angel (or equivalent), 76% superkid
    mohair, 24% silk (218yd/200m per 25g ball)
1[1] x 25g ball in 02 Black (C)
*Rowan Shimmer (or equivalent), 60% cupro,
    40% polyester (191yd/175m per 25g ball)
1[1] x 25g ball in 095 Jet (D)
1 pair each of US10 ½ /11 (7mm) and
    US6 (4mm) needles
2 x brown ¾[⅞]in (2[2.25]cm) diameter buttons
2 x black ½[⅝]in (1.25[1.5]cm) diameter buttons
Small amount of toy stuffing
Stitch holder
Tapestry needle
Sewing needle
Black sewing thread
Thin cardstock to make pompoms
*Use yarn DOUBLED

SIZES

To fit: child up to 8 years [adult]

GAUGE

13 sts and 18 rows to 4in (10cm) over stockinette stitch using US10 ½ /11 (7mm) needles. Use larger or smaller needles if necessary to obtain correct gauge.

FOX CHART (8 rows x 61[65] sts)

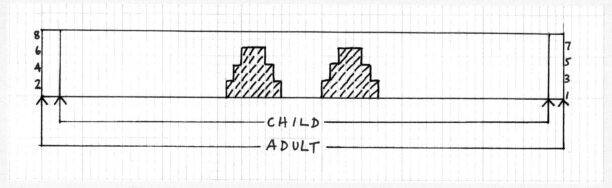

KEY

☐ YARN A
▨ YARN B

OVERVIEW

The fox features are knitted in a simple intarsia pattern, giving a three-dimensional effect, and the little black nose and the ears are worked separately.

MAIN PIECE

First earflap

Both sizes

*With larger needles and A, cast on 3 sts.

Row 1 (inc) (RS): Kfb, k1, kfb (5 sts).

Row 2: K2, p1, k2.

Row 3 (inc): Kfb, k3, kfb (7 sts).

Row 4: K2, p3, k2.

Row 5 (inc): Kfb, k5, kfb (9 sts).

Row 6: K2, p5, k2.

Row 7 (inc): Kfb, k7, kfb (11 sts).

Row 8: K2, p7, k2.

Row 9 (inc): Kfb, k9, kfb (13 sts).

Row 10: K2, p9, k2.

Row 11 (inc): Kfb, k11, kfb (15 sts).

Row 12: K2, p11, k2.

Adult size only

Row 13 (inc): Kfb, k13, kfb (17 sts).

Row 14: K2, p13, k2.

Both sizes

Row 15: Knit.

Row 16: As row 12[14].*

Break yarn and leave these sts on a holder.

Second earflap

Work as given for first earflap from * to *. The following is worked in intarsia:

Next row: Cast on and k 5 sts, knit across 15[17] sts of second earflap, turn. Join in B and cast on 21 sts, turn, knit across 15[17] sts of first earflap in A, turn, cast

on 5 sts in A (61[65] sts).

Next row (WS): K7A, p11[13]A, k2A, k21B, k2A, p11[13]A, k7A.

Next row: K20[22]A, k21B, k20[22]A.

Rep last 2 rows once more.

Next row (WS): P20[22]A, p21B, p20[22]A.

Next row: K20[22]A, k21B, k20[22]A.

Adult size only

Rep last 2 rows once more.

Both sizes

Rep the first of the previous 2 rows once again to end with a WS row.

Work following 8 rows from chart or as given below:

Row 1: K21[23]A, k7B, k5A, k7B, k21[23]A.

Row 2: P21[23]A, p7B, p5A, p7B, p21[23]A.

Row 3: K22[24]A, k5B, k7A, k5B, k22[24]A.

Row 4: P22[24]A, p5B, p7A, p5B, p22[24]A.

Row 5: K23[25]A, k3B, k9A, k3B, k23[25]A.

Row 6: P23[25]A, p3B, p9A, p3B, p23[25]A.

Row 7: Knit with A.

Row 8: Purl with A.

Rep last 2 rows 4 times more.

Shape crown

Row 1 (RS) (dec): K2tog, (k12[13], sl1, k2tog, psso) 3 times, k12[13], k2tog (53[57] sts).

Row 2: Purl.

Row 3 (dec): K2tog, (k10[11], sl1, k2tog, psso) 3 times, k10[11], k2tog (45[49] sts).

Row 4: Purl.

Row 5 (dec): K2tog, (k8[9], sl1, k2tog, psso) 3 times, k8[9], k2tog (37[41] sts).

Row 6: Purl.

Row 7 (dec): K2tog, (k6[7], sl1, k2tog, psso) 3 times, k6[7], k2tog (29[33] sts).

Row 8: Purl.

Row 9 (dec): K2tog, (k4[5], sl1, k2tog, psso) 3 times, k4[5], k2tog (21[25] sts).

Row 10: Purl.

Row 11 (dec): K2tog, (k2[3], sl1, k2tog, psso) 3 times, k2[3], k2tog (13[17] sts).

Adult size only

Row 12: Purl.

Row 13 (dec): K2tog, (k1, sl1, k2tog, psso) 3 times, k1, k2tog (9 sts).

Both sizes

Break yarn and thread through rem sts, draw up tight and fasten off.

EARFLAP FACING (MAKE 2)
Omit if you plan to add knitted lining
With larger needles and A, cast on 3 sts
and work as for earflaps.
Next: Rep rows 15 and 16, 3 more times.
Bind off loosely.

OUTER EAR (MAKE 2)
Both sizes
With larger needles and C DOUBLED, cast
on 3 sts.
Row 1 (inc): Kfb, k1, kfb (5 sts).
Row 2: Purl.
Row 3 (inc): Kfb, k3, kfb (7 sts).
Row 4: Purl.
Row 5 (inc): Kfb, k5, kfb (9 sts).
Row 6: Purl.
Row 7 (inc): Kfb, k7, kfb (11 sts).
Row 8: Purl.
Row 9 (inc): Kfb, k9, kfb (13 sts).
Adult size only
Row 10: Purl.
Row 11 (inc): Kfb, k11, kfb (15 sts).
Row 12: Purl.
Row 13 (inc): Kfb, k13, kfb (17 sts).
Both sizes
Work 5 rows in st st.
Bind off.

INNER EAR (MAKE 2)
Both sizes
With larger needles and A, cast on 3 sts.
Row 1 (inc): Kfb, k1, kfb (5 sts).
Starting with p row, work 3 rows in st st.
Row 5 (inc): Kfb, k3, kfb (7 sts).
Work 3 rows in st st.
Row 9 (inc): Kfb, k5, kfb (9sts).
Work 5[3] rows st st.

Adult size only
Row 13 (inc): Kfb, k7, kfb (11 sts).
Work 5 rows in st st.
Both sizes
Bind off leaving a long length of yarn.

NOSE
Both sizes
Starting at the narrow base of the
nose, with smaller needles and yarn D
DOUBLED, cast on 5 sts.
Row 1 (inc): (K1, kfb) twice, k1 (7 sts).
Row 2: Purl.
Row 3 (inc): K1, (kfb) twice, k1, (kfb)
twice, k1 (11 sts).
Adult size only
Row 4: Purl.
Row 5 (inc): K2, (kfb) twice, k3, (kfb)
twice, k2 (15 sts).
Both sizes
Bind off knitwise.

FINISHING
Using matching yarn, join the back seam.

With right sides together, sew the
earflap facings to the earflaps, starting
and finishing at the edge of the main
section, leaving the overlapping cast-
on edge open. Turn right side out and
slipstitch the open edges to the inside
of the main section.

With right sides together, sew the inner
to the outer ear, leaving lower edge open.
Turn right side out, positioning the inner
ear so it sits centrally with a slight overlap

each side of the larger outer piece. Lightly
stuff, keeping a flattened shape, and
join the bound-off edges. Bring the two
corners of each side from the lower edge
of the ear to the middle to form a bowl
shape. Stitch to hold in place. Attach to
the main section of the hat, stitching all
around the lower shaped ear, which will
help prevent it from flopping over.

Stitch side edges of the nose together
and, folding the piece with the seam at
center back, join the lower narrow cast-on
edge, then the wider bound-off edge.
Attach the nose to the center front of
the hat, just below the point where yarn
B meets yarn A at the center front.

Make two twisted cords using A (see page
118), each measuring 8[12]in (20[30]
cm) long, using 6[8] strands of yarn. Make
two 2[2⅜]in (5[6]cm) pompoms in B (see
page 118) and attach each to one end
of the twisted cord, then stitch the other
end of the cord to the tip of the earflap.
Using sewing thread, place the small black
buttons over the larger brown buttons
and sew in place for the eyes.

LINING THE HAT
See pages 104–109 for how to make
and attach a cozy fleece or knitted lining
for your hat.

lion

The lion's splendid mane is made by working a furlike looped stitch into the main section of the hat. This creates an open weave, but the chunky wool still provides plenty of warmth.

MATERIALS

Erika Knight Fat Maxi Wool (or equivalent), 100%
    pure British wool (87yd/80m per 100g ball)
3[3] x 100g balls in 20 Artisan (A)
Approx. 5yd (4.5m) of any chunky yarn in black
    for nose (B)
1 pair each of US17 (12mm) and
    US10 ½/11 (7mm) needles
2 x brown ¾[⅞]in (2[2.25]cm) diameter buttons
2 x black ½[⅝]in (1.25[1.5]cm) diameter buttons
Stitch holder
Tapestry needle
Sewing needle
Black sewing thread
Thin cardstock to make pompoms

SIZES

To fit: child up to 8 years [adult]

GAUGE

8 sts and 12 rows to 4in (10cm) over stockinette
stitch using US17 (12mm) needles. Use larger
or smaller needles if necessary to obtain correct
gauge.

SPECIAL ABBREVIATIONS

ML: Make loop by winding the yarn around the
right-hand needle and left forefinger clockwise and
then the right-hand needle again counterclockwise,
as normal. The loop is secured by knitting the two
stitches formed on the needle together. See page
116 for full instructions and illustrations.

OVERVIEW

The lion's mane is knitted into the main section of the hat, starting with the earflaps. The looped stitches change the gauge of the work but add to the fullness of the mane. The ears and nose are worked separately and attached to the hat, and then button eyes and pompom-tipped cords are added.

MAIN PIECE

First earflap

Both sizes

*With larger needles and A, cast on 3 sts.
Row 1 (inc) (RS): Kfb, k1, kfb (5 sts).
Row 2: K2, p1, k2.
Row 3 (inc): Kfb, (ML) 3 times, kfb (7 sts).
Row 4: K2, p3, k2.
Row 5 (inc): Kfb, (ML) 5 times, kfb (9 sts).
Row 6: K2, p5, k2.

Adult size only

Row 7 (inc): Kfb, (ML) 7 times, kfb (11 sts).
Row 8: K2, p7, k2.

Both sizes

Row 9: K2, (ML) 5[7] times, k2.
Row 10: As row 6[8].*
Break yarn and leave these sts on a holder.

Second earflap

Work as given for first earflap from * to *.
Next row: Cast on and k 4 sts, (K2, (ML) 5[7] times, k2) of second earflap, turn, cast on 15 sts, turn, (K2, (ML) 5[7] times, k2) of first earflap, turn, cast on 4 sts (41[45] sts).
Next row (WS): K6, p5[7], k19, p5[7], k6.
Next row: K6, (ML) 5[7] times, k19, (ML)

5[7] times, k6.
Rep first of last 2 rows once more.
Next row: K1, (ML) 12[14] times, k15, (ML) 12[14] times, k1.
Next row: Purl.
Rep last 2 rows 2[3] times.

Shape face

Row 1: K1, (ML) 13[15] times, k13, (ML) 13[15] times, k1.
Row 2: Purl.
Row 3: K1 (ML) 14[16] times, k11, (ML) 14[16] times, k1.
Row 4: Purl.
Row 5: K1, (ML) 15[17] times, k9, (ML) 15[17] times, k1.
Row 6: Purl.
Row 7: K1, (ML) to last st, k1.

Shape crown

Row 1 (dec): P0[1], p2tog, (p1, p2tog) to end (27[30] sts).
Row 2: K1, (ML) to last st, k1.
Row 3 (dec): P1[0], (p2tog) to end (14[15] sts).
Break yarn and thread through rem sts, draw up tight and fasten off.

EARFLAP FACINGS (MAKE 2)

Omit if you plan to add knitted lining

Both sizes

With larger needles and A, cast on 3 sts.
Row 1 (inc) (RS): Kfb, k1, kfb (5 sts).
Row 2: K2, p1, k2.
Row 3 (inc): Kfb, k3, kfb (7 sts).
Row 4: K2, p3, k2.
Row 5 (inc): Kfb, k5, kfb (9 sts).
Row 6: K2, p5, k2.

Adult size only

Row 7 (inc): Kfb, k7, kfb (11 sts).

Row 8: K2, p7, k2.

Both sizes

Row 9: Knit.
Row 10: As row 6[8].
Next: Rep rows 9 and 10, 3 more times.
Bind off loosely.

EARS (MAKE 2)

With larger needles and A, cast on 6[7] sts.
Row 1: Knit.
*Row 2 (inc): Kfb, k4[5], kfb (8[9] sts).

Adult size only

Row 3: Knit.
Row 4 (inc): Kfb, k7, kfb (11 sts).

Both sizes

Knit 5 rows.

Adult size only

Next row: Knit.
Next row (dec): K2tog, k7, k2tog (9 sts).
Next row: Knit.

Both sizes

Next row (dec): K2tog, k4[5], k2tog (6[7] sts).
Next row: Knit.*
Rep from * to *. Bind off.

NOSE

Both sizes

Starting at the narrow base of the nose, with smaller needles and yarn B, cast on 3 sts.
Row 1 (WS): Purl.
Row 2 (inc): Kfb, k1, kfb (5 sts).
Row 3: Purl
Row 4 (inc): Kfb, (k1, kfb) twice (8 sts).
Row 5: Purl.

Adult size only

Row 6: Kfb, k6, kfb (10 sts).

Row 7: Purl.

Row 8 (dec): K2tog, k6, k2tog (8 sts).

Row 9: Purl.

Both sizes

Row 10 (dec): K2tog (k1, k2tog) twice (5 sts).

Row 11: Purl.

Row 12 (dec): K2tog, k1, k2tog (3 sts). Bind off.

FINISHING

Make sure the loops don't get caught up in the stitches when making up the hat. Using matching yarn, join the back seam.

With right sides together, sew the earflap facings to the earflaps, starting and finishing at the edge of the main section, leaving the overlapping cast-on edge open. Turn right side out and pin in place, easing in the fullness of the looped

earflap edges to match the facings. Slipstitch the open edges to the inside of the main section.

Fold ear piece with right sides together and join the shaped side seams, leaving the cast-on and bound-off edges open. Turn right sides out, stuff lightly, then close the seam. Fold the lower edge, bringing each corner to the center to shape the ear and stitch in place. Attach the finished ears to the hat.

Fold nose with wrong sides together, matching the narrow cast-on and bound-off edges. Join the seams neatly. Attach the nose to the center front of the hat, with the narrow end sitting just above the garter-stitch edge.

Make two twisted cords using A (see page 118), each measuring 8[12]in (20[30]cm) long, using 4[6] strands of yarn. Make two

2[2³⁄₈]in (5[6]cm) pompoms in A (see page 118) and attach each to one end of the twisted cord, then stitch the other end of the cord to the earflap tip.

Using black sewing thread, place the small black buttons over the larger brown buttons and sew onto the lion's face for the eyes.

LINING THE HAT

See pages 104–109 for how to make and attach a cozy fleece or knitted lining for your hat.

mouse

Yarns of varied textures combine to give the mouse a tactile quality and interesting finish. Be sure to stitch the large ears around the entire lower edge when attaching them to the hat so they don't flop.

MATERIALS

Wendy Merino Chunky (or equivalent), 100%
    merino wool (71yd/65m per 50g ball)
3[3] x 50g balls in 2477 Soot (A)
Wendy Sorrento DK (or equivalent), 45% cotton,
    55% acrylic (159yd/145m per 50g ball)
1[1] x 50g ball in 2405 Pale Pink (B)
Any textured or bouclé chunky yarn
1[1] x 50g ball in light gray (C)
Approx. 4³⁄₈yd (4m) of any worsted yarn in
    black for nose (D)
1 pair each of US10 ¹⁄₂/11 (7mm) and
    US6 (4mm) needles
2 x white ³⁄₄[⁷⁄₈]in (2[2.25]cm) diameter buttons
2 x black ¹⁄₂[⁵⁄₈]in (1.25[1.5]cm) diameter buttons
Stitch holder
Tapestry needle
Sewing needle
Black sewing thread
Thin cardstock to make pompoms
Small amount of toy stuffing

SIZES

To fit: child up to 8 years [adult]

GAUGE

13 sts and 18 rows to 4in (10cm) over stockinette
stitch using US10 ¹⁄₂/11 (7mm) needles. Use
larger or smaller needles if necessary to obtain
correct gauge.

OVERVIEW

The main part of the hat is knitted first, beginning with the earflaps. Ears, cheeks, and the bobble nose are worked separately and stitched to the hat after the back seam is joined and the ear facings attached. Whiskers are embroidered across the cheeks.

MAIN PIECE

First earflap

Both sizes

*With larger needles and A, cast on 3 sts.
Row 1 (inc) (RS): Kfb, k1, kfb (5 sts).
Row 2: K2, p1, k2.
Row 3 (inc): Kfb, k3, kfb (7 sts).
Row 4: K2, p3, k2.

Row 5 (inc): Kfb, k5, kfb (9 sts).
Row 6: K2, p5, k2.
Row 7 (inc): Kfb, k7, kfb (11 sts).
Row 8: K2, p7, k2.
Row 9 (inc): Kfb, k9, kfb (13 sts).
Row 10: K2, p9, k2.
Row 11 (inc): Kfb, k11, kfb (15 sts).
Row 12: K2, p11, k2.

Adult size only

Row 13 (inc): Kfb, k13, kfb (17 sts).
Row 14: K2, p13, k2.

Both sizes

Row 15: Knit.
Row 16: As row 12[14].*
Break yarn and leave these sts on a holder.

Second earflap

Work as given for first earflap from * to *.
Next row: Cast on and k 5 sts, knit across 15[17] sts of second earflap, turn, cast on 21 sts, turn, knit across 15[17] sts of first earflap, turn, cast on 5 sts (61[65] sts).
Next row (WS): K7, p11[13], k25, p11[13], k7.
Next row: Knit.
Rep last 2 rows once more and then, starting with a purl row, work 19[21] rows in st st, ending with a WS row.

Shape crown

Row 1 (RS) (dec): K2tog, (k12[13], sl1, k2tog, psso) 3 times, k12[13], k2tog (53[57] sts).
Row 2: Purl.
Row 3 (dec): K2tog, (k10[11], sl1, k2tog, psso) 3 times, k10[11], k2tog (45[49] sts).
Row 4: Purl.
Row 5 (dec): K2tog, (k8[9], sl1, k2tog, psso) 3 times, k8[9], k2tog (37[41] sts).

Row 6: Purl.
Row 7 (dec): K2tog, (k6[7], sl1, k2tog, psso) 3 times, k6[7], k2tog (29[33] sts).
Row 8: Purl.
Row 9 (dec): K2tog, (k4[5], sl1, k2tog, psso) 3 times, k4[5], k2tog (21[25] sts).
Row 10: Purl.
Row 11 (dec): K2tog, (k2[3], sl1, k2tog, psso) 3 times, k2[3], k2tog (13[17] sts).

Adult size only

Row 12: Purl.
Row 13 (dec): K2tog, (k1, sl1, k2tog, psso) 3 times, k1, k2tog (9 sts).

Both sizes

Break yarn and thread through rem sts, draw up tight and fasten off.

EARFLAP FACING (MAKE 2)

Omit if you plan to add knitted lining
With larger needles and A, cast on 3 sts and work rows 1 to 16 of pattern for earflaps.
Next: Rep rows 15 and 16, 3 more times. Bind off loosely.

EARS (MAKE 4)

With larger needles and A, cast on 7[9] sts.
Rows 1–2: Knit.
Row 3 (inc) (WS): Kfb, k5[7], kfb (9[11] sts).
Row 4 (RS): Knit.
Row 5 (inc): Kfb, k7[9], kfb (11[13] sts).
Row 6: Knit.
Row 7 (inc): Kfb, k9[11], kfb (13[15] sts).
Rows 8–16: Knit.

Adult size only

Rows 17–18: Knit.

Both sizes
Row 19 (dec): K2tog, k9[11], k2tog (11[13] sts).
Row 20: Knit.
Row 21 (dec): K2tog, k7[9], k2tog (9[11] sts).
Row 22: Knit.
Row 23 (dec): K2tog, k5[7], k2tog (7[9] sts).
Row 24: Knit.
Row 25 (dec): K2tog, k3[5], k2tog (5[7] sts).
Cast off.

INNER EARS (MAKE 2)

With smaller needles and B, cast on 7[9] sts and work rows 1 to 24 of ear pattern. Bind off leaving a long length of yarn.

CHEEKS (MAKE 2)

Both sizes
With larger needles and C, cast on 7 sts.
Row 1 (inc): Kfb, k5, kfb (9 sts).
Row 2: Knit.
Row 3 (inc): Kfb, k7, kfb (11 sts).
Rows 4–5: Knit.
Adult size only
Rows 6–7: Knit.
Both sizes
Row 8 (dec): K2tog, k7, k2tog (9 sts).
Row 9: Knit.
Row 10 (dec): K2tog, k5, k2tog (7 sts).
Bind off.

NOSE

Both sizes
Starting at the narrow base of the nose, with smaller needles and D, cast on 3 sts.
Row 1 (inc): Kfb, k1, kfb (5 sts).
Row 2 (inc): K1, (kfb) 3 times, k1 (8 sts).
Adult size only
Row 3 (inc): (K1, kfb) 4 times (12 sts).
Both sizes
Knit 7[9] rows.
Adult size only
Row 13 (dec): (K1, k2tog) 4 times (8 sts).
Both sizes
Next row (dec): K1, (k2tog) 3 times, k1 (5 sts).
Next row (dec): K2tog, k1, k2tog (3 sts). Bind off leaving a long length of yarn. Run a gathering st around the edge and draw up to gather, stuffing the piece to make a ball shape before fastening off.

FINISHING

Using matching yarn, join the back seam.

With right sides together, sew the earflap facings to the earflaps, starting and finishing at the edge of the main section, leaving the overlapping cast-on edge open. Turn right side out and slipstitch the open edges to the inside of the main section.

With right sides together, join the two ear pieces, leaving lower, cast-on edges open. Turn right side out and stuff lightly, then stitch together the cast-on edges. Sew the pink inner pieces to the middle of the ears. Attach the ears in place on the main section of the hat, stitching around the entire lower edges to prevent the ears from flopping over.

Sew cheeks to face, just above the garter-stitch edge, setting them close together.

Stitch the nose between the tops of the cheeks and stitch long whiskers with yarn D across each cheek.

Make two twisted cords in A (see page 118) measuring 8[12]in (20[30]cm), using 6[8] strands of yarn. Make two 2[2⅜]in (5[6]cm) pompoms in C (see page 118) and attach each to one end of the twisted cord, then stitch the other end of the cord to the tip of the earflap.

Using sewing thread, place the small black buttons over the larger white buttons and sew in place for the eyes.

LINING THE HAT

See pages 104–109 for how to make and attach a cozy fleece or knitted lining for your hat.

rabbit

When spring is in the air, this floppy-eared bunny rabbit
will keep the breezes at bay. Fluffy cheeks,
pink nose, and two bunny-tail pompoms
add to his cuddly charm.

MATERIALS

Rowan Felted Tweed Chunky (or equivalent),
    50% merino wool, 25% alpaca, 25% viscose
    (55yd/50m per 50g ball)
4[4] x 50g balls in 280 Sand (A)
1[1] x 50g ball in 290 Candy (B)
Rowan Purelife British Sheep Breeds Bouclé
    (or equivalent), 100% British wool (66yd/60m
    per 100g ball)
1[1] x 100g ball in 220 Blue Faced Leicester/ecru (C)
1 pair each of US10½ (6.5mm) and
    US11 (8mm) needles
2 x white ⅞in (2.25cm) diameter buttons
2 x black ⅝in (1.5cm) diameter buttons
Stitch holder
Tapestry needle
Sewing needle
Black sewing thread
Thin cardstock to make pompoms

SIZES

To fit: child up to 8 years [adult]

GAUGE

12½ sts and 17½ rows to 4in (10cm) over
stockinette stitch using US10½ (6.5mm) needles.
Use larger or smaller needles if necessary to
obtain correct gauge.

OVERVIEW

The long bunny ears, cheeks, and nose are knitted separately and stitched in place to the finished hat. The main part begins with the earflaps, which will warm the wearer's ears. The hat is finished with button eyes and twisted cords decorated with pompoms.

MAIN PIECE

First earflap

Both sizes

*With smaller needles and A, cast on 3 sts.

Row 1 (inc) (RS): Kfb, k1, kfb (5 sts).

Row 2: K2, p1, k2.

Row 3 (inc): Kfb, k3, kfb (7 sts).

Row 4: K2, p3, k2.

Row 5 (inc): Kfb, k5, kfb (9 sts).

Row 6: K2, p5, k2.

Row 7 (inc): Kfb, k7, kfb (11 sts).

Row 8: K2, p7, k2.

Row 9 (inc): Kfb, k9, kfb (13 sts).

Row 10: K2, p9, k2.

Row 11 (inc): Kfb, k11, kfb (15 sts).

Row 12: K2, p11, k2.

Adult size only

Row 13 (inc): Kfb, k13, kfb (17 sts).

Row 14: K2, p13, k2.

Both sizes

Row 15: Knit.

Row 16: As row 12[14].*

Break yarn and leave these sts on a holder.

Second earflap

Work as given for first earflap from * to *.

Next row: Cast on and knit 5 sts, knit across 15[17] sts of second earflap, turn,

cast on 21 sts, turn, knit across 15[17] sts of first earflap, turn, cast on 5 sts (61[65] sts).

Next row (WS): K7, p11[13], k25, p11[13], k7.

Next row: Knit.

Rep last 2 rows once more and then, starting with a purl row, work 19[21] rows in st st, ending with a WS row.

Shape crown

Row 1 (RS) (dec): K2tog, (k12[13], sl1, k2tog, psso) 3 times, k12[13], k2tog (53[57] sts).

Row 2: Purl.

Row 3 (dec): K2tog, (k10[11], sl1, k2tog,

psso) 3 times, k10[11], k2tog (45[49] sts).

Row 4: Purl.

Row 5 (dec): K2tog, (k8[9], sl1, k2tog, psso) 3 times, k8[9], k2tog (37[41] sts).

Row 6: Purl.

Row 7 (dec): K2tog, (k6[7], sl1, k2tog, psso) 3 times, k6[7], k2tog (29[33] sts).

Row 8: Purl.

Row 9 (dec): K2tog, (k4[5], sl1, k2tog, psso) 3 times, k4[5], k2tog (21[25] sts).

Row 10: Purl.

Row 11 (dec): K2tog, (k2[3], sl1, k2tog, psso) 3 times, k2[3], k2tog (13[17] sts).

Adult size only

Row 12: Purl.

Row 13 (dec): K2tog, (k1, sl1, k2tog, psso) 3 times, k1, k2tog (9 sts).

Both sizes

Break yarn and thread through rem sts, draw up tight and fasten off.

EARFLAP FACING (MAKE 2)

Omit if you plan to add knitted lining

With smaller needles and A, cast on 3 sts and work rows 1 to 16 of pattern for earflaps.

Next: Rep rows 15 and 16, 3 more times. Bind off loosely.

OUTER EAR (MAKE 2)

Both sizes

With smaller needles and A, cast on 3 sts.

Row 1 (inc): Kfb, k1, kfb (5 sts).

Row 2: Purl.

Row 3 (inc): Kfb, k3, kfb (7 sts).

Row 4: Purl.

Row 5 (inc): Kfb, k5, kfb (9 sts).

Row 6: Purl.

Row 7 (inc): Kfb, k7, kfb (11 sts).
Row 8: Purl.
Row 9 (inc): Kfb, k9, kfb (13 sts).
Adult size only
Row 10: Purl.
Row 11 (inc): Kfb, k11, kfb (15 sts).
Row 12: Purl.
Row 13 (inc): Kfb, k13, kfb (17 sts).
Both sizes
Work 17 rows in st st.
Bind off.

INNER EAR (MAKE 2)
Both sizes
With smaller needles and B, cast on 3 sts.
Row 1 (inc): Kfb, k1, kfb (5 sts).
Starting with p row, work 3 rows in st st.
Row 5 (inc): Kfb, k3, kfb (7 sts).
Work 3 rows in st st.
Row 9 (inc): Kfb, k5, kfb (9 sts).
Adult size only
Work 3 rows st st.
Row 13 (inc): Kfb, k7, kfb (11 sts).
Both sizes
Work 17 rows in st st.
Bind off leaving a long length of yarn.

CHEEKS (MAKE 2)
Both sizes
With larger needles and C, cast on 3 sts.
Row 1 (inc): Kfb, k1, kfb (5 sts).
Row 2: Knit.
Row 3 (inc): Kfb, k3, kfb (7 sts).
Rows 4–5: Knit.
Row 6 (dec): K2tog, k3, k2tog (5 sts).
Row 7: Knit.
Row 8 (dec): K2tog, k1, k2tog (3 sts).
Bind off.

NOSE
Both sizes
With larger needles and B, cast on 5 sts.
Work 5 rows in st st.
Bind off knitwise.

FINISHING
Using matching yarn, join the back seam.

With right sides together, sew the earflap facings to the earflaps, starting and finishing at the edge of the main section, leaving the overlapping cast-on edge open. Turn right side out and slipstitch the open edges to the inside of the main section.

With right sides together, sew the inner to the outer ear, leaving the lower edge open. Turn right sides out, positioning the inner ear so it sits centrally with a slight overlap each side of the larger outer piece. Join the bound-off edges. Bring the two corners of each side from the lower edge of the ear to the middle to shape. Stitch to hold in place. Attach to the main section of the hat.

Sew cheeks to face, just above the garter-stitch edge, setting them close together.

Fold nose diagonally and join edges to form a triangular shape. With the folded edge at the top, attach nose to center front of hat, between the tops of the cheeks.

Make two twisted cords (see page 118) measuring 8[12]in (20[30]cm) long in A, using 6[8] strands of yarn. Make two 2[2⅜]in (5[6]cm) pompoms (see page 118) in C and attach each to one end of the twisted cord, then stitch the other end of the cord to the tip of the earflap.

Using sewing thread, place the small black buttons over the larger white buttons and sew in place for the eyes.

LINING THE HAT
See pages 104–109 for how to make and attach a cozy fleece or knitted lining for your hat.

cat

Soft, textured bouclé wool makes this cute kitty
oh so cuddly and using super-chunky yarn makes the
hat very quick to knit—purrr-fect!

MATERIALS

Rowan Purelife British Sheep Breeds Bouclé
    (or equivalent), 100% British wool (66yd/60m
    per 100g ball)

1[1] x 100g ball in 223 Dark Brown Masham (A)

1[1] x 100g ball in 220 Blue Faced Leicester/ecru (B)

Approx. 2¾yd (2.5m) of any worsted yarn in pink
    for nose (C)

1 pair each of US10½ (7.5mm), US11 (8mm),
    and US6 (4mm) needles

2 x dark brown ⅞in (2.25cm) diameter buttons

2 x black ⅝in (1.5cm) diameter buttons

Stitch holder

Tapestry needle

Sewing needle

Black sewing thread

Black embroidery thread

Small amount of toy stuffing

SIZES

To fit: child up to 8 years [adult]

GAUGE

8½ sts and 13 rows to 4in (10cm) over
stockinette stitch using US11 (8mm) needles.
Use larger or smaller needles if necessary to
obtain correct gauge.

Work following 8 rows from chart or as given below:

Row 1: K14[16]A, k13B, k14[16]A.
Row 2: P14[16]A, p13B, p14[16]A.
Row 3: K15[17]A, k11B, k15[17]A.
Row 4: P15[17]A, p11B, p15[17]A.
Row 5: K16[18]A, k9B, k16[18]A.
Row 6: P16[18]A, p9B, p16[18]A.
Row 7: K to end in A.
Row 8: P to end in A.

Shape crown

Row 1 (dec): K2tog, (k7[8], sl1, k2tog, psso) 3 times, k7[8], k2tog (33[37] sts).
Row 2: Purl.
Row 3 (dec): K2tog, (k5[6], sl1, k2tog, psso) 3 times, k5[6], k2tog (25[29] sts).
Row 4: Purl.
Row 5 (dec): K2tog, (k3[4], sl1, k2tog, psso) 3 times, k3[4], k2tog (17[21] sts).
Row 6: Purl.
Row 7 (dec): K2tog, (k1[2], sl1, k2tog, psso) 3 times, k1[2], k2tog (9[13] sts).
Break yarn and thread through rem sts, draw up tight and fasten off.

OUTER EAR (MAKE 2)
Both sizes
With larger needles and A, cast on 3 sts.
Row 1 (inc): Kfb, k1, kfb (5 sts).
Row 2: Purl.
Row 3 (inc): Kfb, k3, kfb (7 sts).
Row 4: Purl.
Row 5 (inc): Kfb, k5, kfb (9 sts).
Adult size only
Row 6: Purl.
Row 7 (inc): Kfb, k7, kfb (11 sts).
Both sizes
Work 3 rows in st st. Bind off.

INNER EAR (MAKE 2)
Both sizes
With larger needles and B, cast on 3 sts.
Row 1: Knit.
Row 2: Purl.
Row 3 (inc): Kfb, k1, kfb (5 sts).
Starting with p row, work 5[3] rows in st st.
Adult size only
Row 7 (inc): Kfb, k3, kfb (7 sts).
Work 3 rows in st st.
Both sizes
Bind off leaving a long length of yarn.

CHEEKS (MAKE 2)
Both sizes
Using larger needles and B, cast on 3 sts.
Row 1 (inc): Kfb, k1, kfb (5 sts).
Row 2: Knit.
Row 3 (inc): Kfb, k3, kfb (7 sts).
Row 4: Knit.
Adult size only
Row 5: Knit.
Both sizes
Row 6 (dec): K2tog, k3, k2tog (5 sts).
Row 7: Knit.
Row 8 (dec): K2tog, k1, k2tog (3 sts).
Bind off.

OVERVIEW
The cat hat is worked in intarsia, with the cheeks knitted separately and stitched to the face, giving a little shape to the features. Whiskers are embroidered using long stitches.

MAIN PIECE
With medium-sized needles and A, cast on 41[45] sts.
Work 3 rows in garter st. Change to larger needles.
The following is worked in intarsia:
Next row (RS): K13[15]A, k15B, k13[15]A.
Next row: P13[15]A, p15B, p13[15]A.
Rep last 2 rows 2[3] times.

CAT CHART (8 rows x 41[45] sts)

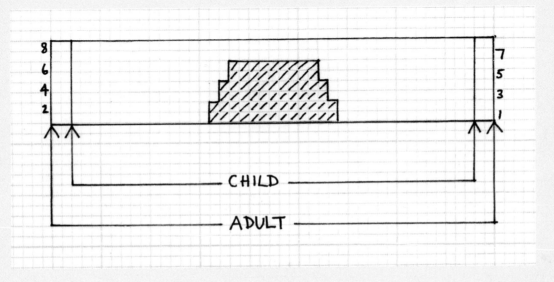

NOSE

Both sizes

Starting at the narrow base of the nose, with smaller needles and yarn C, cast on 3 sts.

Row 1 (inc): Kfb, k1, kfb (5 sts).

Row 2: Purl

Row 3 (inc): (K1, kfb) twice, k1 (7 sts).

Row 4: Purl

Row 5 (inc): K1, (kfb) twice, k1, (kfb) twice, k1 (11 sts).

Adult size only

Row 6: Purl.

Row 7 (inc): K2, (kfb) twice, k3, (kfb) twice, k2 (15 sts).

Both sizes

Bind off knitwise.

FINISHING

Using matching yarn, join the back seam.

With right sides together, sew the inner to the outer ear, leaving lower edge open. Turn right side out, positioning the inner ear so it sits in the center with a slight overlap each side of the larger outer piece. Stuff lightly, keeping the shape flat, and join the bound-off edges. Attach to the main section of the hat. Sew cheeks to face, just over the garter-stitch edge, setting them close together. Stitch the side edges of the nose together and, folding the piece with the seam at center back, join the bound-off edge. With the wide bound-off edge at the top, attach the nose to the face, between the tops of the cheeks.

Embroider whiskers on the cheeks by working long stitches in black embroidery thread or yarn (see page 119). Using sewing thread, place the small black buttons over the larger brown buttons and sew in place for the eyes.

LINING THE HAT

See pages 104–109 for how to make and attach a cozy fleece or knitted lining for your hat.

dog

This loyal pooch has a playful puppy eye patch
and long ears that make this tracker-style hat. It can be
worn with button-up ears as an alerted hound or with
ears down as the earnest investigator.

MATERIALS

Rowan Purelife British Sheep Breeds Chunky
    Undyed (or equivalent), 100% British wool
    (120yd/110m per 100g ball)

1[1] x 100g ball in 950 Blue Faced Leicester (A)

1[1] x 100g ball in 952 Mid Brown Jacob (B)

*Rowan Shimmer (or equivalent), 60% cupro,
    40% polyester (191yd/175m per 25g ball)

1[1] x 25g ball in 095 Jet (C)

1 pair each of US10½ /11 (7mm) and
    US8 (4mm) needles

4 x cream or white ⅞in (2.25cm) diameter buttons

2 x black ⅝in (1.5cm) diameter buttons

Tapestry needle

Sewing needle

Cream or white thread

Black sewing thread

*Use Rowan Shimmer DOUBLED

SIZES

To fit: child up to 8 years [adult]

GAUGE

13 sts and 18 rows to 4in (10cm) over stockinette
stitch using US10½ /11 (7mm) needles. Use
larger or smaller needles if necessary to obtain
correct gauge.

OVERVIEW

The main section starts with knitting the ear facings, then working them into the crown of the hat. The ears, eye patch, and shiny, wet-look nose are knitted separately and stitched on. The long ears can be buttoned up; another set of buttons are attached for the eyes.

EAR FACINGS (MAKE 2)

Both sizes

With larger needles and A, cast on 5 sts.
Row 1 (RS) (inc): Kfb, k3, kfb (7 sts).
Row 2 (inc): Kfb, k5, kfb (9 sts).
Row 3 (inc): Kfb, k7, kfb (11 sts).
Row 4 (inc): Kfb, k9, kfb (13 sts).

Adult size only

Row 5 (inc): Kfb, k11, kfb (15 sts).

Both sizes

Continue in garter st (knit every row) until work measures 4¾[6]in (12[15]cm) from cast-on edge, ending with a WS row. Break yarn and leave sts on a holder.

MAIN PIECE

Using larger needles and A, cast on 8 sts, turn and knit across 13[15] sts of one ear facing, turn and cast on 19 sts, turn and knit across 13[15] sts of other ear facing, turn and cast on 8 sts (61[65] sts).
Work 3 rows in garter st.
Beg with a knit row, work in st st for 20[22] rows, ending with a WS row.

Shape crown

Row 1 (RS) (dec): K2tog, k11[12], sl1, k2tog, psso, (k13[14], sl1, k2tog, psso) twice, k11[12], k2tog (53[57] sts).
Row 2: Purl.
Row 3 (dec): K2tog, k9[10], sl1, k2tog, psso, (k11[12], sl1, k2tog, psso) twice, k9[10], k2tog (45[49] sts).
Row 4: Purl.
Row 5 (dec): K2tog, k7[8], sl1, k2tog, psso, (k9[10], sl1, k2tog, psso) twice, k7[8], k2tog (37[41] sts).
Row 6: Purl.
Row 7 (dec): K2tog, k5[6], sl1, k2tog, psso, (k7[8], sl1, k2tog, psso) twice, k5[6], k2tog (29[33] sts).
Row 8: Purl.
Row 9 (dec): K2tog, k3[4], sl1, k2tog, psso, (k5[6], sl1, k2tog, psso) twice, k3[4], k2tog (21[25] sts).
Row 10: Purl.
Row 11 (dec): K2tog, k1[2], sl1, k2tog, psso, (k3[4], sl1, k2tog, psso) twice, k1[2], k2tog (13[17] sts).

Adult size only

Row 12: Purl.
Row 13 (dec): K2tog, sl1, k2tog, psso, (k2, sl1, k2tog, psso) twice, k2tog (9 sts).

Both sizes

Break yarn and thread through rem sts, draw up tight and fasten off.

EARS (MAKE 2)

Both sizes

With larger needles and B, cast on 3 sts, (pass previous st over st just made, slipping it off the needle, cast on 1) 3 times to make buttonhole.
Row 1 (WS): K1, turn, cast on 3 sts, turn, k1 (5 sts).
Row 2: (inc): Kfb, k3, kfb (7 sts).
Row 3 (inc): Kfb, k5, kfb (9 sts).
Row 4 (inc): Kfb, k7, kfb (11 sts).
Row 5 (inc): Kfb, k9, kfb (13 sts).

Adult size only

Row 6 (inc): Kfb, k11, kfb (15 sts).

Both sizes

Continue in garter st until work measures 7[8¼]in (18[21]cm) from cast-on edge of row 1, ending with a WS row.

Shape top

Next row (dec): K1, k2tog, k to last 3 sts, k2tog, k1.
Next row: Knit.
Rep last 2 rows until 9 sts rem, then rep the first of the last 2 rows twice more (5 sts).
Next row (dec): K1, sl1, k2tog, psso, k1 (3 sts).
Bind off 3 sts.

NOSE

Both sizes

Starting at the narrow base of the nose, with smaller needles and yarn C DOUBLED, cast on 7 sts.

Row 1 (RS): Knit.

Row 2: Purl.

Row 3 (inc): K1, (kfb) twice, k1, (kfb) twice, k1 (11 sts).

Adult size only

Row 4: Purl.

Row 5 (inc): K2, (kfb) twice, k3, (kfb) twice, k2 (15 sts).

Both sizes

Bind off knitwise.

PATCH

With larger needles and B, cast on 5[7] sts.

Rows 1–2: Knit.

Row 3 (inc): Kfb, k3[5], kfb (7[9] sts).

Row 4: Knit.

Row 5 (inc): Kfb, k5[7], kfb (9[11] sts).

Rows 6–10: Knit.

Adult size only

Knit 4 rows.

Both sizes

Next row (dec): K2tog, k5[7], k2tog (7[9] sts).

Next row: Knit.

Next row (dec): K2tog, k3[5], k2tog (5[7] sts).

Next 2 rows: Knit.

Bind off.

FINISHING

Using matching yarn, join the back seam of main section.

Position the wrong side of ears over right side of facings and hat. Slipstitch in place, leaving the buttonholes free.

Sew eye patch to front of main section. Stitch side edges of nose together and, folding the piece with the seam at center back, join the lower narrow cast-on edge, then the wider cast-off edge. Attach the nose to the center front of the hat, just above the garter-stitch edge.

Using sewing thread, sew a cream button to each of the tops of the ears. Place the black buttons over the remaining cream buttons and stitch to the main section for the eyes.

LINING THE HAT

See pages 104–109 for how to make and attach a cozy fleece or knitted lining for your hat.

koala

This cuddly koala has a snuggly embrace and bobble ears—just imagine the furry creature atop a eucalyptus tree. Long pompom-tipped ties add length and height as the bear clings to its holding place.

MATERIALS

Wendy Merino Chunky (or equivalent), 100%
   merino wool (71yd/65m per 50g ball)
3[3] x 50g balls in 2472 Pumice (A)
1[1] x 50g ball in 2470 Cloud (B)
Wendy Merino Bliss DK (or equivalent), 100%
   merino wool (126yd/116m per 50g ball)
1[1] x 50g ball in 2366 Jet (C)
1 pair each of US10 ½/11 (7mm) and
   US6 (4mm) needles
2 x brown ¾[⅞]in (2[2.25]cm) diameter buttons
2 x black ½[⅝]in (1.25[1.5]cm) diameter buttons
Small amount of toy stuffing
Stitch holder
Tapestry needle
Sewing needle
Black sewing thread
Thin cardstock to make pompoms

SIZES

To fit: child up to 8 years [adult]

GAUGE

13 sts and 18 rows to 4in (10cm) over stockinette
stitch using US10 ½/11 (7mm) needles. Use
larger or smaller needles if necessary to obtain
correct gauge.

OVERVIEW

The triangular shaped earflaps are worked first and joined at the lower edge of the crown of the hat. Ear facings are knitted to line the earflaps. Pompoms form the koala's ears, with another pair decorating the ends of the twisted cords that are attached to the tips of the earflaps. A large, stuffed nose and button eyes finish the bear.

MAIN PIECE
First earflap
Both sizes
*With larger needles and A, cast on 3 sts.
Row 1 (inc) (RS): Kfb, k1, kfb (5 sts).
Row 2: K2, p1, k2.
Row 3 (inc): Kfb, k3, kfb (7 sts).
Row 4: K2, p3, k2.
Row 5 (inc): Kfb, k5, kfb (9 sts).

Row 6: K2, p5, k2.
Row 7 (inc): Kfb, k7, kfb (11 sts).
Row 8: K2, p7, k2.
Row 9 (inc): Kfb, k9, kfb (13 sts).
Row 10: K2, p9, k2.
Row 11 (inc): Kfb, k11, kfb (15 sts).
Row 12: K2, p11, k2.
Adult size only
Row 13 (inc): Kfb, k13, kfb (17 sts).
Row 14: K2, p13, k2.
Both sizes
Row 15: Knit.
Row 16: As row 12[14].*
Break yarn and leave these sts on a holder.

Second earflap
Work as given for first earflap from * to *.
Next row: Cast on and k 5 sts, knit across 15[17] sts of second earflap, turn, cast on

21 sts, turn, knit across 15[17] sts of first earflap, turn, cast on 5 sts (61[65] sts).
Next row (WS): K7, p11[13], k25, p11[13], k7.
Next row: Knit.
Rep last 2 rows once more and then, starting with a purl row, work 19[21] rows in st st, ending with a WS row.
Shape crown
Row 1 (RS) (dec): K2tog, (k12[13], sl1, k2tog, psso) 3 times, k12[13], k2tog (53[57] sts).
Row 2: Purl.
Row 3 (dec): K2tog, (k10[11], sl1, k2tog, psso) 3 times, k10[11], k2tog (45[49] sts).
Row 4: Purl.
Row 5 (dec): K2tog, (k8[9], sl1, k2tog, psso) 3 times, k8[9], k2tog (37[41] sts).
Row 6: Purl.

Row 7 (dec): K2tog, (k6[7], sl1, k2tog, psso) 3 times, k6[7], k2tog (29[33] sts).
Row 8: Purl.
Row 9 (dec): K2tog, (k4[5], sl1, k2tog, psso) 3 times, k4[5], k2tog (21[25] sts).
Row 10: Purl.
Row 11 (dec): K2tog, (k2[3], sl1, k2tog, psso) 3 times, k2[3], k2tog (13[17] sts).
Adult size only
Row 12: Purl.
Row 13 (dec): K2tog, (k1, sl1, k2tog, psso) 3 times, k1, k2tog (9 sts).
Both sizes
Break yarn and thread through rem sts, draw up tight and fasten off.

EARFLAP FACING (MAKE 2)
Omit if you plan to add knitted lining
With larger needles and A, cast on 3 sts and work rows 1–16 of pattern for earflaps.
Next: Rep rows 15 and 16, 3 more times. Bind off loosely.

NOSE
Using smaller needles and C, cast on 18[21] sts.
Beg with a knit row, work 1⅝[2]in (4[5])cm in st st, ending with a purl row.
Shape top
Next row (RS) (dec): (K1, k2tog) 6[7] times (12[14] sts).
Next row: Purl.
Next row (dec): (k2tog) 6[7] times (6[7] sts).
Next row: Purl.
Break yarn and thread through rem sts, draw up tight and fasten off.

FINISHING
Using matching yarn, join the back seam.

With right sides together, sew the earflap facings to the earflaps, starting and finishing at the edge of the main section, leaving the overlapping cast-on edge open. Turn right side out and slipstitch the open edges to the inside of the main section.

Join seam of the nose and stuff the piece lightly. With the seam at the center back of the work, slipstitch the cast-on edge together to join. Attach the nose to the main part of the hat at the center front, just above the garter-stitch border. With B, make two pompom ears (see page 118) measuring 2⅜[3]in (6[7.5]cm) across. Stitch to each side of the hat at the beginning of shaping. Make two twisted cords using A (see page 118), each measuring 8[12]in (20[30]cm) long, using 6[8] strands of yarn. Make two 2[2⅜]in (5[6]cm) pompoms in A and attach each to one end of the twisted cord, then stitch the other end of the cord to the tip of the earflap.

Using sewing thread, place the small black buttons over the larger brown buttons and sew in place for the eyes.

LINING THE HAT
See pages 104–109 for how to make and attach a cozy fleece or knitted lining.

panda

A cuddly creature in striking black and white, this cute
panda bear is easy to knit in chunky yarn; his distinct
features make him an instantly recognizable and
warm addition to your winter wardrobe.

MATERIALS

Wendy Mode Chunky (or equivalent), 50% pure
   merino wool, 50% fine acrylic (153yd/140m
   per 100g ball)
1[1] x 100g balls in 201 Whisper White (A)
1[1] x 100g ball in 220 Coal (B)
1 pair of US10½/11 (7mm) needles
2 x white ¾[⅞]in (2[2.25]cm) diameter buttons
2 x black ½[⅝]in (1.25[1.5]cm) diameter buttons
Small amount of toy stuffing
Stitch holder
Tapestry needle
Sewing needle
Black sewing thread
Thin cardstock to make pompoms

SIZES

To fit: child up to 8 years [adult]

GAUGE

13 sts and 18 rows to 4in (10cm) over stockinette
stitch using US10½/11 (7mm) needles. Use larger
or smaller needles if necessary to obtain correct
gauge.

OVERVIEW

The main part of the hat is decorated with eye patches, large round ears, and a nose, which are all knitted separately. Button eyes finish off the features and pompoms are attached to twisted cords, which hang from each earflap.

MAIN PIECE
First earflap
Both sizes
*With larger needles and A, cast on 3 sts.
Row 1 (inc) (RS): Kfb, k1, kfb (5 sts).
Row 2: K2, p1, k2.
Row 3 (inc): Kfb, k3, kfb (7 sts).
Row 4: K2, p3, k2.
Row 5 (inc): Kfb, k5, kfb (9 sts).
Row 6: K2, p5, k2.
Row 7 (inc): Kfb, k7, kfb (11 sts).
Row 8: K2, p7, k2.
Row 9 (inc): Kfb, k9, kfb (13 sts).
Row 10: K2, p9, k2.
Row 11 (inc): Kfb, k11, kfb (15 sts).
Row 12: K2, p11, k2.
Adult size only
Row 13 (inc): Kfb, k13, kfb (17 sts).
Row 14: K2, p13, k2.
Both sizes
Row 15: Knit.
Row 16: As row 12[14].*
Break yarn and leave these sts on a holder.
Second earflap
Work as given for first earflap from * to *.

Next row: Cast on and k 5 sts, knit across 15[17] sts of second earflap, turn, cast on 21 sts, turn, knit across 15[17] sts of first earflap, turn, cast on 5 sts (61[65] sts).
Next row (WS): K7, p11[13], k25, p11[13], k7.
Next row: Knit.
Rep last 2 rows once more and then, starting with a purl row, work 19[21] rows in st st, ending with a WS row.
Shape crown
Row 1 (RS) (dec): K2tog, (k12[13], sl1, k2tog, psso) 3 times, k12[13], k2tog (53[57] sts).
Row 2: Purl.
Row 3 (dec): K2tog, (k10[11], sl1, k2tog, psso) 3 times, k10[11], k2tog (45[49] sts).
Row 4: Purl.
Row 5 (dec): K2tog, (k8[9], sl1, k2tog, psso) 3 times, k8[9], k2tog (37[41] sts).
Row 6: Purl.
Row 7 (dec): K2tog, (k6[7], sl1, k2tog, psso) 3 times, k6[7], k2tog (29[33] sts).
Row 8: Purl.
Row 9 (dec): K2tog, (k4[5], sl1, k2tog, psso) 3 times, k4[5], k2tog (21[25] sts).
Row 10: Purl.
Row 11 (dec): K2tog, (k2[3], sl1, k2tog, psso) 3 times, k2[3], k2tog (13[17] sts).
Adult size only
Row 12: Purl.
Row 13 (dec): K2tog, (k1, sl1, k2tog, psso) 3 times, k1, k2tog (9 sts).

Both sizes
Break yarn and thread through rem sts, draw up tight and fasten off.

EARFLAP FACING (MAKE 2)
Omit if you plan to add knitted lining
With larger needles and A, cast on 3 sts and work rows 1–16 of pattern for earflaps.
Next: Rep rows 15 and 16, 3 more times. Bind off loosely.

EYE PATCHES (MAKE 2)
Both sizes
With larger needles and B, cast on 5 sts.
Rows 1-2: Knit.
Row 3 (inc): Kfb, k3, kfb (7 sts).
Adult size only
Row 4: Knit.
Row 5 (inc): Kfb, k5, kfb (9 sts).
Both sizes
Rows 6-12: Knit.
Adult size only
Rows 13-16: Knit.
Row 17 (dec): K2tog, k5, k2tog (7 sts).
Row 18: Knit.
Both sizes
Row 19 (dec): K2tog, k3, k2tog (5 sts).
Rows 20-21: Knit.
Bind off.

EARS (MAKE 2)

With larger needles and B, cast on 7[9] sts.

Rows 1–2: Knit.

Row 3 (inc): Kfb, k5[7], kfb (9[11] sts).

Adult size only

Row 4: Knit.

Row 5 (inc): Kfb, k9, kfb (13 sts).

Both sizes

Rows 6–10: Knit.

Adult size only

Rows 11–12: Knit.

Row 13 (dec): K2tog, k9, k2tog (11 sts).

Row 14: Knit.

Both sizes

Row 15 (dec): K2tog, k5[7], k2tog (7[9] sts).

Row 16: Knit.

Row 17 (dec): K2tog, k3[5], k2tog (5[7] sts).

Rows 18: Knit.

Row 19 (inc): Kfb, k3[5], kfb (7[9] sts).

Rows 20–36: As rows 2–16.

Knit 1 row.

Bind off.

NOSE

Both sizes

Starting at the narrow base of the nose, with larger needles and yarn B, cast on 3 sts.

Row 1 (RS): Knit.

Row 2: Purl.

Row 3 (inc): (Kfb) 3 times (6 sts).

Row 4: Purl.

Adult size only

Row 5 (inc): (Kfb) 6 times (12 sts).

Row 6: Purl.

Row 7 (dec): (K2tog) 6 times (6 sts).

Row 8: Purl.

Both sizes

Row 9 (dec): (K2tog) 3 times (3 sts).

Row 10: Purl.

Row 11: Knit.

Bind off knitwise.

FINISHING

Using matching yarn, join the back seam.

With right sides together, sew the earflap facings to the earflaps, starting and finishing at the edge of the main section, leaving the overlapping cast-on edge open. Turn right side out and slipstitch the open edges to the inside of the main section.

Fold nose with wrong sides together, matching the cast-on and bound-off edges. Join the seams neatly. Attach the nose to the center front of the hat, with the narrow end sitting just above the garter-stitch edge.

Fold ear with right sides together and join the shaped side seams, leaving the cast-on and bound-off edges open. Turn right side out, stuff lightly then close the seam. Fold the lower edge, bringing each corner to the center to shape the ear and stitch in place. Attach the ears to each side of the hat about one third of the way from the beginning of the shaping.

Make two twisted cords using A (see page 118), each measuring 8[12]in (20[30]cm) long, using 6[8] strands of yarn. Make two 2[2⅜]in (5[6]cm) pompoms in B (see page 118) and attach each to one end of the twisted cord, then stitch the other end of the cord to the tip of the earflap.

Using sewing thread, place the small black buttons over the larger white buttons and sew onto the panda's patches for eyes.

LINING THE HAT

See pages 104–109 for how to make and attach a cozy fleece or knitted lining for your hat.

COW

The markings on this hat can be placed anywhere to make your Holstein-Friesian unique. You can easily create another breed, such as a Jersey, by substituting a shade of light brown for the cream and black.

MATERIALS

Debbie Bliss Rialto Chunky (or equivalent), 100%
    merino wool (65yd/60m per 50g ball)
3[3] x 50g balls in 003 Ecru (A)
1[2] x 50g balls in 006 Camel (B)
2[2] x 50g balls in 001 Black (C)
1 pair of US10½/11 (7mm) needles
2 x brown ⅞[1⅛]in (2.25[2.75]cm) diameter
    buttons
4 x black ½[⅝]in (1.25[1.5]cm) diameter buttons
Small amount of toy stuffing
Stitch holder
Tapestry needle
Sewing needle
Black sewing thread
Thin cardstock to make tassels

SIZES

To fit: child up to 8 years [adult]

GAUGE

13 sts and 18 rows to 4in (10cm) over
stockinette stitch using US10½/11 (7mm)
needles. Use larger or smaller needles if
necessary to obtain correct gauge.

OVERVIEW

The main part of the hat is knitted in stockinette stitch, then the features that create the finished look are knitted and attached. The ears are knitted in two pieces and sewn together, bringing the corners of the lower edges to the center to form the shape. The curved horns are created by increasing and decreasing stitches, and garter-stitch patches are positioned randomly over the hat.

MAIN PIECE

First earflap

Both sizes

*With larger needles and A, cast on 3 sts.
Row 1 (inc) (RS): Kfb, k1, kfb (5 sts).
Row 2: K2, p1, k2.
Row 3 (inc): Kfb, k3, kfb (7 sts).
Row 4: K2, p3, k2.
Row 5 (inc): Kfb, k5, kfb (9 sts).
Row 6: K2, p5, k2.
Row 7 (inc): Kfb, k7, kfb (11 sts).
Row 8: K2, p7, k2.
Row 9 (inc): Kfb, k9, kfb (13 sts).
Row 10: K2, p9, k2.
Row 11 (inc): Kfb, k11, kfb (15 sts).
Row 12: K2, p11, k2.

Adult size only

Row 13 (inc): Kfb, k13, kfb (17 sts).
Row 14: K2, p13, k2.

Both sizes

Row 15: Knit.
Row 16: As row 12[14].*
Break yarn and leave these sts on a holder.

Second earflap

Work as given for first earflap from * to *.
Next row: Cast on and k 5 sts, knit across 15[17] sts of second earflap, turn, cast on 21 sts, turn, knit across 15[17] sts of first earflap, turn, cast on 5 sts (61[65] sts).
Next row (WS): K7, p11[13], k25, p11[13], k7.
Next row: Knit.
Rep last 2 rows once more and then, starting with a purl row, work 19[21] rows in st st, ending with a WS row.

Shape crown

Row 1 (RS) (dec): K2tog, (k12[13], sl1, k2tog, psso) 3 times, k12[13], k2tog (53[57] sts).
Row 2: Purl.
Row 3 (dec): K2tog, (k10[11], sl1, k2tog, psso) 3 times, k10[11], k2tog (45[49] sts).
Row 4: Purl.
Row 5 (dec): K2tog, (k8[9], sl1, k2tog, psso) 3 times, k8[9], k2tog (37[41] sts).
Row 6: Purl.
Row 7 (dec): K2tog, (k6[7], sl1, k2tog, psso) 3 times, k6[7], k2tog (29[33] sts).
Row 8: Purl.
Row 9 (dec): K2tog, (k4[5], sl1, k2tog, psso) 3 times, k4[5], k2tog (21[25] sts).
Row 10: Purl.
Row 11 (dec): K2tog, (k2[3], sl1, k2tog, psso) 3 times, k2[3], k2tog (13[17] sts).

Adult size only

Row 12: Purl.
Row 13 (dec): K2tog, (k1, sl1, k2tog, psso) 3 times, k1, k2tog (9 sts).

Both sizes

Break yarn and thread through rem sts, draw up tight and fasten off.

EARFLAP FACING (MAKE 2)

Omit if you plan to add knitted lining
With larger needles and A, cast on 3 sts and work as for earflaps.
Next: Rep rows 15 and 16, 3 more times. Bind off loosely.

OUTER EAR (MAKE 2)

Both sizes

With larger needles and C, cast on 3 sts.
Row 1 (inc): Kfb, k1, kfb (5 sts).
Row 2: Purl.
Row 3 (inc): Kfb, k3, kfb (7 sts).
Row 4: Purl.
Row 5 (inc): Kfb, k5, kfb (9 sts).
Row 6: Purl.
Row 7 (inc): Kfb, k7, kfb (11 sts).
Row 8: Purl.
Row 9 (inc): Kfb, k9, kfb (13 sts).

Adult size only

Row 10: Purl.
Row 11 (inc): Kfb, k11, kfb (15 sts).

Both sizes

Work 9 rows in st st.
Bind off.

INNER EAR (MAKE 2)

Both sizes

With larger needles and C, cast on 3 sts.
Work as given for outer ear.

NOSE

With larger needles and B, cast on
15[17] sts.
Work 8[10] rows in garter stitch.
Next row (WS) (dec): K2tog, k11[13],
k2tog (13[15] sts).
Next row: Knit.
Next row (dec): K2tog, k9[11] k2tog
(11[13] sts).
Next row: Knit.
Next row (dec): K2tog, k7[9], k2tog
(9[11] sts).
Bind off.

PATCHES (MAKE 4)
Both sizes
With larger needles and C, cast on 5 sts.
Row 1 (inc): Kfb, k3, kfb (7 sts).
Row 2: Knit.
Row 3 (inc): Kfb, k5, kfb (9 sts).
Adult size only
Row 4: Knit.
Row 5 (inc): Kfb, k7, kfb (11 sts).
Both sizes
Knit 5[7] rows.
Next row (dec): K2tog, k5[7], k2tog
(7[9] sts).
Next row: Knit.
Next row (dec): K2tog, k3[5], k2tog
(5[7] sts).
Knit 6 rows.
Next row (dec): K2tog, k1[3], k2tog
(3[5] sts). Bind off.

HORNS (MAKE 2)
With larger needles and B DOUBLED, cast
on 11[15] sts.

Row 1 (dec): K2tog, k to last 2 sts, k2tog
(9[13] sts).
Row 2: Purl.
Adult size only
Row 3 (dec): K2tog, k to last 2 sts, k2tog
(11 sts).
Row 4: Purl.
Both sizes
Row 5: Kfb, k2[3], sl1, k2tog, psso,
k2[3], kfb.
Row 6: Purl.
Rep rows 5 and 6 once[twice] more.
Next row (dec): K3[4], sl1, k2tog, psso,
k3[4] (7[9] sts).
Next row: Purl.
Next row (dec): K2tog, k0[1], sl 1, k2tog,
psso, k0[1], k2tog (3[5] sts).
Break yarn and thread through rem sts,
draw up tight and fasten off.

FINISHING
Using matching yarn, join the back seam.

With right sides together, sew the
earflap facings to the earflaps,
starting and finishing at the edge of
the main section and leaving the
overlapping cast-on edge open. Turn
right side out and slipstitch the open
edges to the inside of the main section.

Join the curved seam of the horns. Stuff
firmly and attach to the top of the hat,
curving them in toward each other.

With right sides together, join the two
ear pieces, leaving the lower edge open.

Turn right sides out and join the bound-
off edges. Bring the two corners of each
side from the lower edge of the ear to
the middle to form a bowl shape. Stitch to
hold in place. Attach to the main section
of the hat, next to each horn, stitching all
around the lower shaped ear.

Stitch the nose in place on the front of
the hat with the cast-on edge sitting
just above the rows of garter stitch,
leaving an opening for stuffing. Stuff
lightly to create some shape. Close the
opening and fasten off neatly.

Sew the patches in place to the main
section, positioning them around the
front and back of the hat.

Make two twisted cords using A (see
page 118), each measuring 8[12]in
(20[30]cm), using 6[8] strands of yarn.
Make two tassels (see page 119)
measuring 4[5⅛]in (10[13]cm) long
in C, and attach each to one end of the
twisted cord, then stitch the other end
of the cord to the tip of the earflap.
Using sewing thread, place the small
black buttons over the larger brown
buttons and sew in place for the eyes.
Sew the remaining small black buttons
in place for the nostrils.

LINING THE HAT
See pages 104–109 for how to make
and attach a cozy fleece or knitted lining
for your hat.

lining your hat

sewing in a fleece lining

This lining can be added to any of the hats in this book to make them even cozier. Polar fleece is recommended, but jersey or terry cloth fabrics can also be used.

MATERIALS

22 x 22in (56 x 56cm)
[25 x 25in (63.5 x 63.5cm)]
   polar fleece fabric
Matching thread
Needle
Dressmaking pins
³⁄₈in (1cm) gridded pattern paper
   (or access to a photocopier)
Pencil
Scissors

PATTERN NOTE

This pattern was designed using metric measurements. Although imperial equivalents are given, it may be easiest to work in the metric system while making the lining.

OVERVIEW

1 Using the pattern templates on page 106, scale them to the size that you require (adult- or child-sized), either by transferring onto gridded pattern paper or by photocopying at 200 percent.

2 Cut out the paper pattern following the unbroken lines. Seam allowances of ⁵⁄₈in (1.5cm) are included in the pattern with the stitches indicated as a broken line inside the continuous black outline.

3 Fold the fabric at a 45-degree angle to find the bias. This is the diagonal line that cuts across the warp and the weft, or the vertical and horizontal threads of the fabric (see drawing opposite).

4 Place the pattern on the folded fleece so the arrow of the grainline on the paper follows the direction of the vertical threads of the fabric to allow some elasticity in the finished lining. Be sure the fold marked on the pattern is placed exactly on the bias fold of the fabric. Pin the pattern in place and cut out the fleece.

5 Stitch the darts where indicated on the pattern template. Pin the main seam along the broken line and stitch together. Cut notches into the curved edge (see opposite) and trim the seam.

6 Turn under a hem of ⁵⁄₈in (1.5cm) and pin the lining to the inside of the finished hat, just above the cast-on stitches, with the main seam matching the back seam of the hat. Ease the fabric evenly around the lower edge. Slipstitch the fleece lining in place. Make a few stitches through the top of the crown into the knitted hat to keep it in place.

FINDING THE BIAS

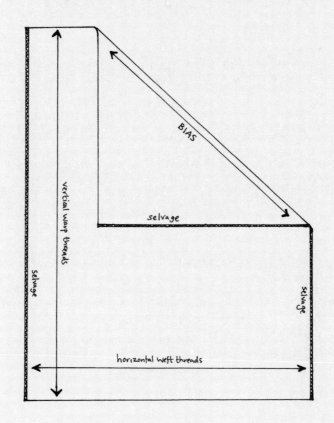

BIAS

vertical warp threads

selvage

selvage

selvage

horizontal weft threads

CUTTING NOTCHES

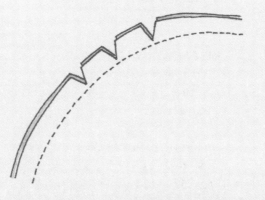

PATTERN TEMPLATE
1 square = ⅜ in (1cm)

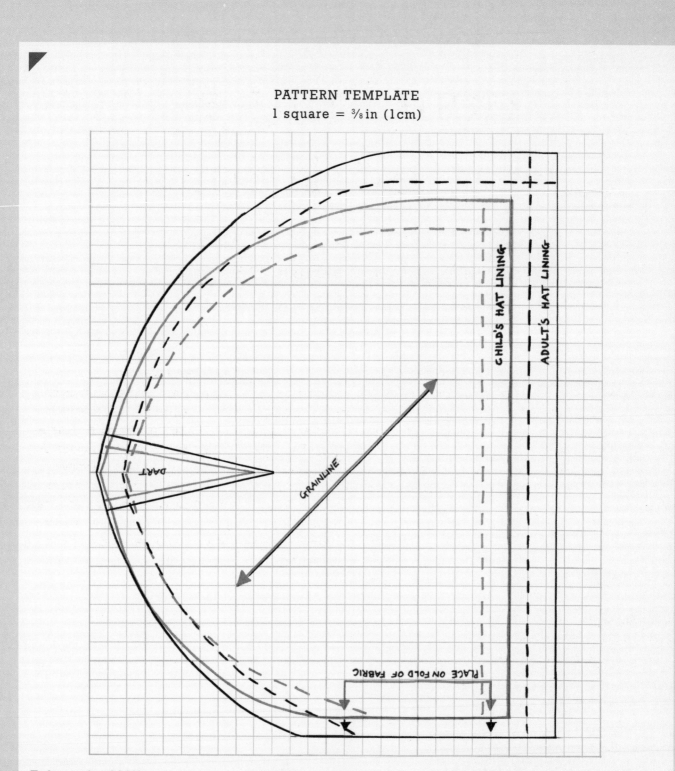

CHILD'S HAT LINING

ADULT'S HAT LINING

DART

GRAINLINE

PLACE ON FOLD OF FABRIC

Enlarge by 200% on a photocopier. ◤ Align marker with arrow on top left of photocopier glass.

inserting a knitted lining

A knitted lining is a cozy alternative to using fleece. It can either be worked in the same shade as your animal hat or in a contrasting color.

MATERIALS

Approx. 3½oz (100g) of yarn used
   for chosen animal hat (A)
Please see chosen animal hat
   pattern for needle sizes required
Stitch holder
Tapestry needle

SIZE
To fit: child up to 8 years [adult]

GAUGE
See chosen animal hat pattern
   for required gauge

OVERVIEW

The knitted lining is worked in the same yarn as the animal hat you are making, so refer to the pattern for the yarn type, needles required, and gauge. The earflap facings are worked first, where applicable, and then the main part of the lining is continued in stockinette stitch. The back seam is joined and the lining slipped inside the hat and stitched in place before finishing with twisted cords and tassels or pompoms, if using.

PATTERN NOTE

Since earflap facings are worked into the knitted lining pattern, omit them where applicable from the main animal pattern when knitting the outer section of the hat, except for those of the Dog and Penguin. The lining is stitched in place after the features are added to the main part of the hat. If twisted cords are to be attached to the earflaps, the knitted lining should go in first.

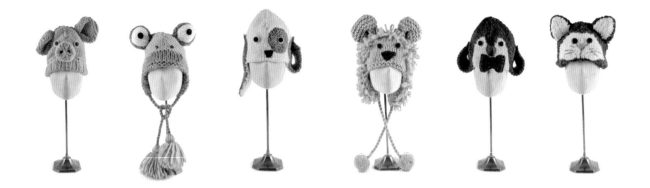

KNITTED LINING FOR RABBIT, CHICKEN, COW, ELEPHANT, FOX, KOALA, MONKEY, MOUSE, AND PANDA

First earflap facing

Both sizes

*With appropriate larger size needles (see hat pattern) for Monkey, Rabbit, Chicken, Cow, Elephant, Fox, Koala, Mouse, or Panda and A, cast on 3 sts.

Row 1 (inc) (RS): Kfb, k1, kfb (5 sts).

Row 2: K2, p1, k2.

Row 3 (inc): Kfb, k3, kfb (7 sts).

Row 4: K2, p3, k2.

Row 5 (inc): Kfb, k5, kfb (9 sts).

Row 6: K2, p5, k2.

Row 7 (inc): Kfb, k7, kfb (11 sts).

Row 8: K2, p7, k2.

Row 9 (inc): Kfb, k9, kfb (13 sts).

Row 10: K2, p9, k2.

Row 11 (inc): Kfb, k11, kfb (15 sts).

Row 12: K2, p11, k2.

Adult size only

Row 13 (inc): Kfb, k13, kfb (17 sts).

Row 14: K2, p13, k2.

Both sizes

Row 15: Knit.

Row 16: As row 12[14].*

Break yarn and leave sts on a holder.

Second earflap facing

Work as given for first earflap from * to *.

Next row: Cast on and k 5 sts, knit across 15[17] sts of second earflap, turn, cast on 21 sts, turn, knit across 15[17] sts of first earflap, turn, cast on 5 sts (61[65] sts).

Next row (WS): K7, p11[13], k25, p11[13], k7.

Next row: Knit.

Rep last 2 rows once more and then, starting with a purl row, work 19[21] rows in st st, ending with a WS row.

Shape crown

Row 1 (RS) (dec): K2tog, (k12[13], sl1, k2tog, psso) 3 times, k12[13], k2tog (53[57] sts).

Row 2: Purl.

Row 3 (dec): K2tog, (k10[11], sl1, k2tog, psso) 3 times, k10[11], k2tog (45[49] sts).

Row 4: Purl.

Row 5 (dec): K2tog, (k8[9], sl1, k2tog, psso) 3 times, k8[9], k2tog (37[41] sts).

Row 6: Purl.

Row 7 (dec): K2tog, (k6[7], sl1, k2tog, psso) 3 times, k6[7], k2tog (29[33] sts).

Row 8: Purl.

Row 9 (dec): K2tog, (k4[5], sl1, k2tog, psso) 3 times, k4[5], k2tog (21[25] sts).

Row 10: Purl.

Row 11 (dec): K2tog, (k2[3], sl1, k2tog, psso) 3 times, k2[3], k2tog (13[17] sts).

Adult size only

Row 12: Purl.

Row 13 (dec): K2tog, (k1, sl1, k2tog, psso) 3 times, k1, k2tog (9 sts).

Both sizes

Break yarn and thread through rem sts, draw up tight and fasten off.

KNITTED LINING FOR PIG

With larger needles (see hat pattern) and A, cast on 61[65] sts.

Starting with a knit row, work in st st for 16[18] rows, ending with a WS row.

Shape crown

Work as for Rabbit, Chicken, Cow, Elephant, Fox, Koala, Monkey, Mouse, and Panda.

KNITTED LINING FOR DOG AND PENGUIN

With larger needles (see hat pattern) and A, cast on 61[65] sts.

Work 3 rows in garter st.

Starting with a knit row, work in st st for 20[22] rows, ending with a WS row.

Shape crown

Row 1 (RS) (dec): K2tog, k11[12], sl1, k2tog, psso, (k13[14], sl1, k2tog, psso) twice, k11[12], k2tog (53[57] sts).

Row 2: Purl.

Row 3 (dec): K2tog, k9[10], sl1, k2tog, psso, (k11[12], sl1, k2tog, psso) twice, k9[10], k2tog (45[49] sts).

Row 4: Purl.

Row 5 (dec): K2tog, k7[8], sl1, k2tog, psso, (k9[10], sl1, k2tog, psso) twice, k9[8], k2tog (37[41] sts).

Row 6: Purl.

Row 7 (dec): K2tog, k5[6], sl1, k2tog, psso, (k7[8], sl1, k2tog, psso) twice, k5[6], k2tog (29[33] sts).

Row 8: Purl.

Row 9 (dec): K2tog, k3[4], sl1, k2tog, psso, (k5[6], sl1, k2tog, psso) twice, k3[4], k2tog (21[25] sts).

Row 10: Purl.

Row 11 (dec): K2tog, k1[2], sl1, k2tog, psso, (k3[4], sl1, k2tog, psso) twice, k1[2], k2tog (13[17] sts).

Adult size only

Row 12: Purl.

Row 13 (dec): K2tog, sl1, k2tog, psso, (k2, sl1, k2tog, psso) twice, k2tog (9 sts).

Both sizes

Break yarn and thread through rem sts, draw up tight and fasten off.

KNITTED LINING FOR FROG AND LION

First earflap facing

Both sizes

*With appropriate larger size needles (see hat pattern) and A, cast on 3 sts.

Row 1 (inc) (RS): Kfb, k1, kfb (5 sts).

Row 2: K2, p1, k2.

Row 3 (inc): Kfb, k3, kfb (7 sts).

Row 4: K2, p3, k2.

Row 5 (inc): Kfb, k5, kfb (9 sts).

Row 6: K2, p5, k2.

Adult size only

Row 7 (inc): Kfb, k7, kfb (11 sts).

Row 8: K2, p7, k2.

Both sizes

Row 9: Knit

Row 10: As row 6 [8].*

Break yarn and leave these sts on a holder.

Second earflap facing

Work as given for first earflap from * to *.

Next row: Cast on and k 4 sts, knit across 9[11] sts of second earflap, turn, cast on 15 sts, turn, knit across 9[11] sts of first earflap, turn, cast on 4 sts (41[45] sts).

Next row (WS): K6, p5[7], k19, p5[7], k6.

Next row (RS): Knit.

Rep first of last 2 rows once more. Starting with a knit row, work 16 rows in st st, ending with a purl row.

Shape crown

Row 1 (dec) (RS): K2tog, (k7[8], sl1, k2tog, psso) 3 times, k7[8], k2tog (33[37] sts).

Row 2: Purl.

Row 3 (dec): K2tog, (k5[6], sl1, k2tog, psso) 3 times, k5[6], k2tog (25[29] sts).

Row 4: Purl.

Row 5 (dec): K2tog, (k3[4], sl1, k2tog, psso) 3 times, k3[4], k2tog (17[21] sts).

Row 6: Purl.

Row 7 (dec): K2tog, (k1[2], sl1, k2tog, psso) 3 times, k1[2], k2tog (9[13] sts).

Break yarn and thread through rem sts, draw up tight and fasten off.

KNITTED LINING FOR CAT

With medium size needles (see hat pattern) and A, cast on 41[45] sts.
Work 3 rows in garter st.
Change to larger needles.
Starting with a knit row, work 14[16] rows in st st.

Shape crown

Work as for Frog and Lion.

FINISHING

Using matching yarn, join the back seam. With wrong sides together, pin the lining in place inside the main part of the hat and slipstitch neatly around the lower edges. For the Dog and Penguin, pin in position matching lower edges and keeping the lining straight across the earflap facings before stitching. For the Pig, slipstitch the lower edge of the lining to the first row of stockinette stitch after the rib on the main part. Work a few stitches into the top of the crown to keep the lining from slipping.

basic techniques

getting started

When starting a new project, always read the materials list at the beginning of the pattern carefully to see what you will need to gather together.

SIZING

The finished animal hats are intended to fit children up to 8 years of age and adults. They should fit an average size head. See "Reading patterns."

GAUGE

Checking the gauge before starting a project is vital as this will affect the size and look of the finished piece. The gauge is the number of rows and stitches per square inch or centimeter of knitted fabric. A knitted sample should be big enough to enable you to measure easily—around 5in (13cm) square.

Using the same needles and stitch that the gauge has been measured over in the pattern, knit a sample then lay it out on a flat surface. Place a ruler horizontally across the work and mark 4in (10cm) with pins. Count the number of stitches between the pins, including half stitches. This will give you the gauge of knitting.

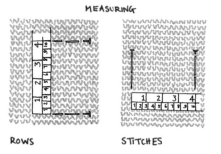

MEASURING

ROWS   STITCHES

Measure the gauge of rows by placing a ruler vertically over the work and mark 4in (10cm) with pins. Count the number of rows between the pins. If the numbers are greater than those stated in the pattern, your gauge is tighter and you should use larger needles. If the number of stitches and rows is less than those stated in the pattern, your gauge is looser, so use smaller needles.

SUBSTITUTING YARNS

When substituting yarns, it is important to calculate the number of balls required by the number of yards or meters per ball rather than the weight of the yarn, as this varies according to the fiber. Gauge is also important. Work a gauge swatch in the yarn you wish to use before starting a project.

READING PATTERNS

The animal hat patterns are written for children's and adults' sizes. The children's size is given first and where the adults' instructions differ, the adjustment is given inside square [ ] brackets. If 0 appears in the instructions, then no stitches or rows are to be worked for this size. Where there is no bracket after the stitches or rows given, the instructions refer to both of the sizes.

READING CHARTS

Each square of a chart represents one stitch and each horizontal row represents one row of knitting. The changes of color or pattern are shown as actual color or symbols. Read the chart from the bottom row to the top, working from right to left for right-side rows and from left to right for wrong-side rows.

knitting basics

All the knitting basics you will need are clearly explained here, from casting on and binding off to sewing up seams and making pompoms.

SLIP KNOT

The first stitch on the needle is the slip knot or slip loop.

1 Form the end of the yarn into a loop. Insert the needle through the loop, catching the long end that is attached to the ball, and draw it back through.

2 Keeping the yarn looped on the needle, pull through until the loop closes around the needle, making sure it is not tight. Pulling on the short end of yarn will loosen the knot, while pulling on the long end will tighten it.

CABLE CAST-ON

This produces a corded foundation row, suitable for items that require an elastic but firm edge.

1 With the slip knot on the left-hand needle, insert the right-hand needle and pass the yarn under and over the point.

2 Pull this loop just made through the stitch.

3 Pass the loop onto the left-hand needle.

4 For the third and following stitches, insert the right-hand needle between the two stitches on the left-hand needle; pass the yarn around the point of the right-hand needle to make a loop and pull through to the front of the work. Pass the loop onto the left-hand needle.

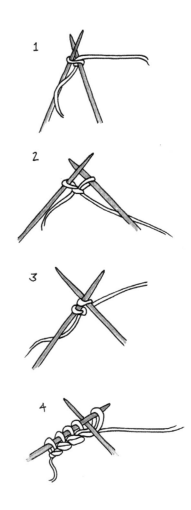

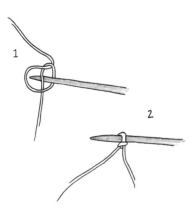

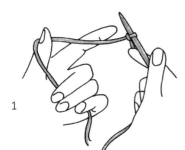

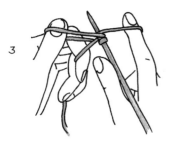

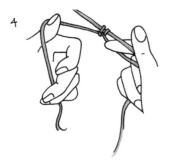

THUMB METHOD

This edge is worked toward the end of the yarn rather than the ball as in the previous method, so be sure to allow enough length at the beginning.

1 Make a slip knot, leaving a long length of yarn. Hold the needle in the right hand and with the length of yarn in the left, pass it around the left thumb and hold in place with the fingers.

2 Insert the needle under and up through the loop on the thumb.

3 With the right hand, pass the yarn from the ball up and over the point of the needle.

4 Draw the yarn through the loop on the thumb, forming the new stitch on the needle. Remove the thumb from the loop and pull on the end of the yarn to tighten the stitch.

KNIT STITCH

This stitch creates a reversible fabric of garter stitch when worked on every row. Each stitch is worked from the left-hand needle to the right-hand needle to form a row of knitting. Then the work is turned and the needles are swapped to the opposite hands to begin another row.

1 Insert the right-hand needle through the first stitch on the left-hand needle, from front to back.

2 Pass the yarn around the point of the right-hand needle.

3 Draw the loop through the stitch, thus forming the new stitch on the right-hand needle.

4 Slip the original stitch off the left-hand needle. Continue in this manner for each remaining stitch.

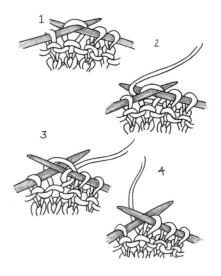

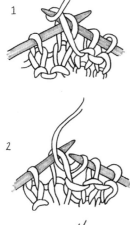

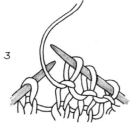

PURL STITCH

The purl stitch is the reverse of the knit stitch. The stitch on the left-hand needle is slipped off to the front of the work. If the purl stitch is used on every row, the effect will be the same as the knit stitch, creating a garter-stitch fabric. By alternating rows of knit and purl, stockinette-stitch fabric is produced. A rib is formed by alternating knit and purl stitches.

1 With the yarn at the front of the work, insert the right-hand needle through the first stitch, from back to front. Pass the yarn in a counterclockwise direction around the point of the right-hand needle.

2 Draw the loop through the stitch, forming the new stitch on the right-hand needle.

3 Slip the original stitch off the left-hand needle. Continue in this manner for each remaining stitch.

GARTER STITCH

Knit every row.

STOCKINETTE STITCH

Row 1 (RS): Knit.
Row 2 (WS): Purl.
Repeat rows 1 and 2 to form the stockinette stitch.

REVERSE STOCKINETTE STITCH

This is the reverse side of the stockinette stitch, where the purl rows are on the right side of the fabric.
Row 1 (RS): Purl.
Row 2 (WS): Knit.
Repeat rows 1 and 2 to form the reverse stockinette stitch.

GARTER STITCH

STOCKINETTE STITCH

REVERSE STOCKINETTE

LOOP STITCH

In steps 1 and 2, the yarn is wound in a figure-eight direction to create two loops on the right-hand needle. The yarn that has been wound around the finger creates the finished loop of the mane.

1 Insert the right-hand needle into the next stitch, holding the left forefinger behind the right-hand needle. Wind the yarn in a clockwise direction over the right-hand needle and forefinger once.

2 Now wind the yarn around the right-hand needle as usual, in a counterclockwise direction, and knit the stitch, keeping the forefinger in the loop.

3 Slip both stitches just made back onto the left-hand needle and knit them together through the back loops.

4 Remove the finger from the loop. Pull the loop to the front of the work before starting the next stitch.

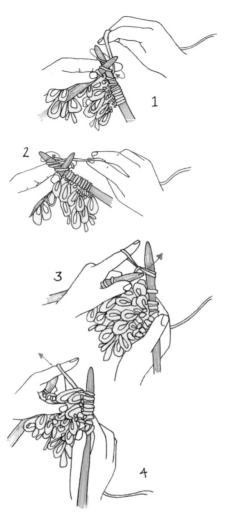

BINDING OFF

Binding off keeps the stitches from unraveling and creates a neat edge. It is important not to bind off too tightly so the work has some elasticity.

Binding off knitwise

1 Knit two stitches. Insert the point of the left-hand needle into the first stitch worked and pass it over the second stitch and off the right-hand needle.

2 One stitch is now on the right-hand needle. Knit the next stitch so there are two stitches on the right-hand needle and pass the first stitch over the second and off the needle as before. Repeat until there is just one stitch remaining. Break the yarn and draw through the last stitch to fasten off.

Binding off purlwise

To bind off in purl, work as for knitwise, working in purl stitch instead of knit.

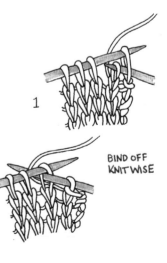

BIND OFF KNITWISE

INTARSIA

The intarsia technique uses blocks of color to create a pattern. Small balls of yarn are used for each area of color. Yarns are twisted as they meet and are changed at the back of the work, rather than being carried across the entire row.

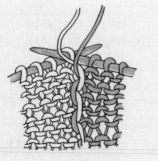

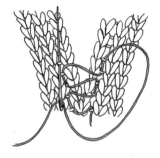

MATTRESS STITCH

SEAMS

Seams should be joined using a blunt-ended tapestry needle and matching yarn, preferably a long length that has been left at the beginning or end of the work since it is already fastened in place. If you are joining in new yarn to sew the pieces together, leave a length at the beginning that can be woven in afterward to prevent any untidy ends showing. Make sure any patterns and shapings are aligned.

Mattress stitch

Mattress stitch produces an invisible seam that is suitable for stockinette-stitch fabric. The finish is neat and straight. Place the two pieces side by side with right sides of work facing you. Insert the needle under two horizontal bars between the first two stitches on one side, then under the same bars on the other piece. Continue picking up the stitches and drawing the edges together every few stitches to join the seam.

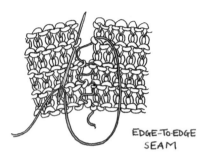

EDGE-TO-EDGE SEAM

Edge-to-edge seam

This is a suitable method for garter-stitch fabric and is also perfect for joining delicate articles as it creates a flat seam with elasticity. Place the two pieces of work together with the edges meeting and the right sides facing you. Join the seam by picking up a loop from the edge of each side alternately.

Slipstitch

Insert the needle into a stitch on the wrong side of the knitting and then into a stitch on the cast-on or bound-off edge. Repeat to the end, keeping the stitches even and not too tight.

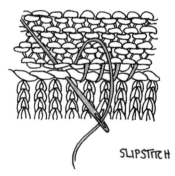

SLIPSTITCH

Backstitch seam

It is important to make sure your stitches are neat and worked in a straight line. The backstitched seam gives a tailored finish to the work.

1 With right sides together and working one stitch in from the edge, begin by working a couple of stitches over each other to secure the seam.

2 Bring the needle through to the front of the work one stitch ahead of the last stitch made. Insert the needle back through the work at the end of the last stitch. Repeat this step to complete the seam.

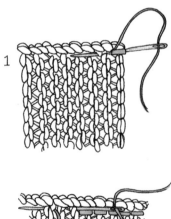

1

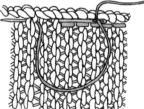

2

finishing touches

Pompoms and tassels are sewn to the ends of hat ties for decoration as well as added weight. Adding features with embroidery gives unique character to the animals.

TWISTED CORD

1 Measure the required number of strands and lengths of yarn and knot them together at the ends. Slip one end over a hook or doorknob and insert a pencil into the other end and hold between the thumb and forefinger, keeping the yarn taut. Turn the pencil clockwise to twist the strands.

2 Continue turning the pencil until the strands are tightly twisted. Fold them, allowing the two halves to twist together naturally. Remove the pencil and carefully undo the knots. With a strand of yarn threaded onto a needle, wind the yarn around the cord near the end and secure with a few stitches. Alternatively, the end can remain knotted but will be bulkier.

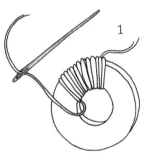

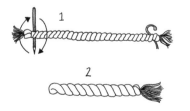

POMPOMS

1 Cut two circles of cardstock to the required measurement for each pompom. Make a hole in the center of each circle. The hole should be about a third of the size of the finished pompom. Thread a tapestry needle with a long length of doubled yarn and, with the two circles held together, wind the yarn through the hole and around the outer edge of the circle. Continue in this way, using new lengths of yarn when needed, until the hole is filled and the circle is covered.

2 Cut through the yarn around the outer edge between the two circles of cardstock. Tie a length of yarn securely around the middle leaving long ends, which will be used to attach the pompoms to the cords. Remove the cardstock and trim the pompom, fluffing it into shape.

TASSELS

1 Cut a piece of cardstock to the required length of the finished tassel. Wind the yarn around the cardstock to the desired thickness. Break yarn, leaving a long length, and thread it through a tapestry needle. Slip the needle through all the loops on the cardstock and tie the yarn tightly at the top edge.

2 Remove the cardstock and wind the yarn around the loops, a little way down from the tied top end, securing them with a few stitches; draw the needle through to the top and leave an end to stitch to the cord. Cut through the folded lower edge and trim to neaten the ends.

FRENCH KNOTS

1 Thread a tapestry needle with a length of yarn. Bring the yarn through to the right side of the work where the knot is to be made and hold it down with the left thumb. Wind the yarn twice around the needle, still holding it firmly in place.

2 Insert the needle back into the work, close to the point where the yarn first came through. Pull the yarn through to tighten the knot and then fasten off or bring the needle back through to the front of the work at the point where you wish to start another French knot.

EMBROIDERING WHISKERS

With the chosen shade of yarn threaded onto a tapestry needle, secure the end at the back of the work near the nose.

1 Bring the needle through to the front at the point near the nose where you want the whisker to start. Insert the needle back into the work at the point where you want the whisker to end, making one long stitch.

2 Bring the needle through to the front at the point where you want the second whisker to end. Insert the needle back into the work at the point where you want the second whisker to begin, near the nose, making one long stitch.

3 Repeat step 1 to complete the third whisker. Fasten off.

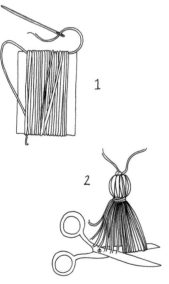

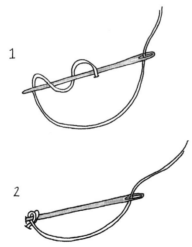

ABBREVIATIONS

alt	alternate	pfb	purl into front and back of next st
approx	approximately		
beg	beginning	psso	pass slipped stitch over
cm	centimeter(s)		
cont	continue	pwise	purlwise
dec	decrease	rem	remaining
foll	following	rep	repeat
g-st	garter stitch	RH	right hand
in	inch(es)	RS	right side
inc	increase by working into front and back of same stitch	sl	slip
		sl st	slip stitch
		st(s)	stitch(es)
K	knit	st st	stockinette stitch
k2tog	decrease by knitting two stitches together	tbl	through back of the loop
kfb	increase by working into front and back of same stitch	tog	together
		WS	wrong side
		yf	yarn forward
kwise	knitwise	*	work instructions immediately following *, then rep as directed
MC	main color		
meas	measures		
ML	make loop	( )	rep instructions inside brackets as many times as instructed
P	purl		
p2tog	purl 2 together		
p2togtbl	purl 2 together through the back loops		
patt	pattern		

CONVERSIONS

Knitting needle sizes

US	Metric	UK
0	2mm	14
1	2.5mm	13
2	2.75mm	12
-	3mm	11
3	3.25mm	10
4	3.5mm	-
5	3.75mm	9
6	4mm	8
7	4.5mm	7
8	5mm	6
9	5.5mm	5
10	6mm	4
10½	6.5mm	3
-	7mm	2
-	7.5mm	1
11	8mm	0
13	9mm	00
15	10mm	000

US/UK yarn weights

US	UK
Lace	2-ply
Fingering	3-ply
Sport	4-ply
Light worsted	Double knitting (DK)
Fisherman/worsted	Aran
Bulky	Chunky
Extra bulky	Super chunky

SUPPLIERS

YARNS

Deramores
(Stockists of Erika Knight,
Twilleys, and Wendy yarns)
Units 5–9 Tomas Seth Business Park
Argent Road
Queenborough
UK
ME11 5TS
Tel: +44 (0)8455 194573
www.deramores.com
Delivery available to the US

Knitting Fever Inc.
(Distributors of Debbie Bliss,
Sirdar, and Sublime yarns)
315 Bayview Avenue
Amityville
New York
NY 11701
Tel: 1 516 546 3600
www.knittingfever.com

Westminster Fibers
(Distributors of Rowan yarns)
165 Ledge Street
Nashua
NH 03060
Tel: 1 (800) 445 9276
www.westminsterfibers.com

BUTTONS

Blumenthal Lansing
One Palmer Terrace
Carlstadt
NJ 07072
Tel: 1 (800) 553 4158
www.blumenthallansing.com

JHB International Inc.
1955 South Quince Street
Denver
CO 80231
Tel: 1 (800) 525 9007
www.buttons.com

YARN SOURCES

We have tried to supply sources for each of the yarns specified. However, you may wish to substitute a yarn that is available locally or at retail stores such as Hobby Lobby, Jo-Ann fabric, Michael's stores, Target, or Wal-Mart.

Find your local yarn shop:
www.sweaterbabe.com/directory
www.knitmap.com
www.yarngroup.org

Hobby Lobby   www.hobbylobby.com
Jo-Ann fabric and craft stores
     www.joann.com
Michael's stores   www.michaels.com
Target   www.Target.com
Wal-Mart   www.walmart.com

If you are substituting brands of yarn, be sure to do a gauge swatch. Yarn companies Bernat, Caron, Lion Brand Yarn, Patons, and Red Heart all offer helpful information on yarn substitution.

Bernat   www.bernat.com
Caron   www.caron.com
Lion Brand Yarn   www.lionbrand.com
Patons   www.patonsyarns.com
Red Heart   www.redheart.com

ABOUT THE AUTHOR

Vanessa Mooncie spent many happy hours as a child with her mother and grandmother, learning how to knit and crochet. She went on to study fashion and textile design and became a self-employed children's wear designer, illustrator and interior designer. She now specializes in silkscreen work and designing crochet jewelry through her company Kissy Suzuki (www.kissysuzuki.com). She lives with her family in a rural village in the south of England. Vanessa is also the author of *Crocheted Accessories* for GMC Publications and is a regular contributor to other craft books and magazines.

AUTHOR'S ACKNOWLEDGMENTS

Thank you to my family for all their patience and support, especially Honey and Dolly—avid wearers of animal hats!

PUBLISHER'S ACKNOWLEDGMENTS

GMC Publications would like to thank the following people for their help in creating this book.

Main photography: Chris Gloag
Still life photography: Rebecca Mothersole
Model: Vanessa Grasse at Zone models
Hair and makeup: Jeni Dodson
Pattern checking: Jude Roust
Illustrations: Vanessa Mooncie

INDEX

To place an order or to request a catalog, contact
The Taunton Press, Inc.
63 South Main Street, P.O. Box 5506, Newtown, CT 06470-5506

www.taunton.com